MULTICULTURAL
BABY
NAMES

5,000 AFRICAN, ARABIC, ASIAN, HAWAIIAN, HISPANIC, INDIAN, AND NATIVE AMERICAN NAMES

M.J. ABADIE

LONGMEADOW
P R E S S

Dedicated to my nieces and nephew
Megan Elizabeth Abadie
Caroline Rose Abadie
Kathleen Victoria Abadie
Charles Hedrick Abadie

Cover design by Kelvin P. Oden
Interior design by Guenet Abraham
Library of Congress Cataloging-in-Publication Data

Abadie, M. J.
    Multicultural baby names / by M. J. Abadie. —1st ed.
        p.   cm.
    ISBN 0-681-45232-3
    1. Names, Personal—Dictionaries.   I. Title.
CS2377.A23   1993
929.4'4'03—dc20   93-26226
                                                                    CIP

Printed in United States of America
First Edition
0 9 8 7 6 5 4 3 2 1

ACKNOWLEDGEMENTS

My thanks go to my editor, Pamela Liflander, for her superior advice and consent, making the work a pleasant and rewarding experience.

My sincere appreciation to Ji Sun Chang, of the Korea Society, for patiently explaining the complex process of name choosing in Korean society and providing examples.

Thanks also to the As-Suq Booksellers of Brooklyn, NY for generously allowing me their library.

And, last but not least, I would like to thank all the previous researchers in this endlessly fascinating field whose work has provided a reservoir of valuable information.

$\mathscr{C}$ONTENTS

Foreword
vii

African Names
1

Arabic Names
48

Chinese Names
84

Japanese Names
116

Korean Names
137

Vietnamese Names
144

Hindu Names
149

Hispanic Names
168

Native American Names
210

Hawaiian Names
237

$\mathcal{F}$OREWORD

Could anyone, writing in English, compiling a book of baby names, fail to recall Juliet's lament, so poignantly penned by Shakespeare?

What's Montague? It is nor hand, nor foot
Nor arm, nor face, nor any other part
Belonging to a man. O, be some other name.
What's in a name? That which we call a rose
By any other name would smell as sweet.

These immortal words have echoed down to the English-speaking world over the centuries, influencing the choosing of names and promoting a widespread attitude that any name is as good as any other. Is it true?

Not in traditional non-English-speaking cultures. In Africa, Asia and Hawaii; to followers of the Muslim and Hindu faith; and to Native American tribes and Hispanics the choosing of a name for a child is a matter of great importance and enduring significance.

Trends in naming children change. Names that were popular just a few years ago are now out of fashion, and names that once were considered to reflect the highest of human virtues (such as Prudence or Chastity) are now mostly unused or faintly ridiculous-sounding to modern ears.

Of all current trends, the most obvious is the dipping into traditional name pools from a culture in which the parents have their own roots.

The melting pot of America continues to absorb people from other nationalities and cultures, enriching society with the traditions of their individual systems of name choosing.

This book enables parents of non-European backgrounds to explore their cultural roots when choosing names for their children—the citizens of the 21st century's Global Village.

M.J. Abadie
1993

*A*FRICAN *N*AMES

In addition to the long history of creating unique names for children, today Americans of African descent are seeking to reconnect the umbilical cord between themselves and their motherland by giving their children the traditional names of Africa.

When a child in a traditional African culture is given a name, it reflects a complex set of ideas about the world, especially the world of nature. Thus a traditional African name signifies religious as well as personal identity. The community relies on names as an integral part of the process of building and moulding the character of the young. Through the process of naming, an individual is linked both to his ancestors and the spirital or natural world.

For example, the Yoruba people follow the custom of naming a boy on his ninth day of life, a girl on her seventh, and twins on their eighth. Prior to the naming ceremony, which is held at the parent's home, the child is called simply Ikoko Omon, or newborn child.

During the naming ritual, the baby's mouth is touched with a number of substances: water, salt, red pepper, honey, oil, koala nut. These substances symbolize the hoped-for characteristics or virtues of: purity, power, good character, happiness, prosperity, and good fortune, respectively.

After the ceremony, the child's name is announced

to the assembled family and community of guests and feasting and dancing follow, often lasting through the night and into the next day.

In the Ugandan tradition, great importance is given to a child's name, which may indicate the birth order, life circumstances, a specific hope, or the clan's totem (an animal or plant identifying different tribes in larger kingdoms).

An African name creates a continuity with the child and his past, identifying him with his ancestral roots.

Some Facts About Africa

The second largest continent on the globe, Africa, in the wake of its colonial history, now boasts fifty sovereign states.

Bounded on the north by the Mediterranean Sea, its most northerly point is Cape Blanc. The northwest coast is separated from Europe by the Strait of Gibraltar, and it is joined on the northeast to Asia at the Sinai Penisula.

Africa's most easterly point is Cape Hafun and on its east coast are the Red Sea and Indian Ocean with the chief island of Madagascar. To the south it is on the Indian and Atlantic Oceans with the most southerly point at Cape Agulhas.

On the west coast is the Atlantic, there a subdivision of the Gulf of Guinea, and the most westerly point is Cape Vert.

The Atlas Mountains are in the northwest, the high plateau region of Ethiopia in the northeast, and the famous peaks Mount Kenya and Kilimanjaro are in the east.

The great Sahara Desert is in the north; the Kalahari Desert is in the south; and the smaller Libyan and Nubian Deserts of Egypt border the Nile Valley in the northeast.

ᴀFRICA

Female

Name	Meaning	Country or Region of Origin
Aba	Thursday born	Western
Abayomi	Pleasant meeting	Nigeria
Abbo	Vegetable	Uganda
Abebi	We asked for her	Western
Abeke	Petted one	Yoruba
Abena	Tuesday born	Ghana
Abeo	Happiness bringer	Nigeria
Abikanile	Listen	Malani
Abimbola	Born to be rich	Nigeria
Ada	First daughter	Western
Adamna	Beautiful daughter	Nigeria
Adero	Giver of life	Central
Adesimbo	Noble birth	Nigeria
Adong	Absent father	Eastern
Adwoa	Monday born	Ghana
Afiya	Health	Tanzania
Afryea	Born in good times	Ghana
Afua	Friday born	Ghana
Ain	Eye, hence precious	Northern
Aisha	Life bringer	Eastern
Aiyetoro	Peace on earth	Western
Akili	Wisdom	Western
Akosua	Sunday born	Ghana
Akwete	Elder of twins	Ghana

Akwokwo	Younger of twins	Ghana
Ama	Saturday born	Ghana
Amadi	General rejoicing	Nigeria
Aminah	Honest, faithful	Northern
Amira	Queen	Northern
Anan	Fourth born	Western
Anuli	Joy	Western
Asesimba	Noble birth	Western
Asha	Life	Eastern
Atsufi	Twin born	Western
Ayah	Bright	Western
Ayo	Joy	Western
Ayobami	Blessed with joy	Western
Azisa	Precious beauty	Western

. . . .

Babirye	First of twins	Uganda
Bagamba	Ignore ill talk	Uganda
Bahati	Luck	Eastern
Baingama	Equality	Uganda
Bakhitah	Fortunate	Northern
Banasa	Monday born	Western
Beesigye	Trust in god	Uganda
Bejide	Born in rainy season	Nigeria
Bimkubwa	Great lady	Eastern
Binta	Beautiful daughter	Western
Birungi	Nice and pretty	Uganda
Bolade	Honor arrives	Nigeria
Bolanile	Wealth of our house	Western
Boniswa	Revelation	Southern
Borishade	Respects the gods	Western
Bunmi	My gifts	Western
Bupe	Hospitality	Western

• •

Camara	Teacher	Western
Charakupa	Gifted	Western
Chausiku	Night born	Eastern
Chiamaka	Splendid	Western
Chijioke	Owner of gifts	Western
Chiku	Chatterer	Eastern
Chimwala	Stone	Malini
Chinasaokuru	God answers for me	Western
Chinue	God's blessing	Nigeria
Chioneso	Guiding light	Southern
Chipo	Great gift	Southern
Chizoba	Protected (by God)	Western
Chuike	Peace in trouble	Eastern
Chuma	Riches	Southern

• •

Dada	Curly hair	Western
Daib	Excellent	Western
Dalila	Gentle	Eastern
Dalili	Sign or omen	Eastern
Dalmar	Versatile	Western
Damamli	Beautiful vision	Eastern
Dara	Beautiful	Nigeria
Dayo	Joy arrives	Western
Deka	She who pleases	Western
Dembe	Peace	Uganda
Doto	Second of twins	Western
Dridzienyo	A good birth	Western
Dyese	She is my fortune	Central
Dzidzo	Happiness	Western
Dzigbodi	Patience	Western
Dziko	The world	Southern

••••••••••••••••••••••••••••••••••

Ebere	Mercy	Western
Ebun	Gift or boon	Nigeria
Edem	Dedicated to Ndem	Western
Edenausegboye	Good deeds	Nigeria
Efia	Friday born	Ghana
Efioanwan	Born on market day	Western
Efua	Born on Friday	Western
Eka	Mother of the earth	Western
Ekaghogho	Born on important day	Nigeria
Ekanem	Mother of all	Western
Ekechi	God's creation	Western
Ekedinna	Eke is good	Western
Ekellot	Girl after twins	Uganda
Elewechi	We await God	Western
El-Jamah	Paradise	Northern
Elon	God loves me	Western
Emojung	Little old one	Uganda
Enam	God gave her to me	Western
Enomwoyi	One who has grace	Nigeria
Eshe	Life	Eastern
Esi	Sunday born	Western
Esinam	God has heard me	Western
Ewunike	Like a fragrance	Eastern
Ezigbo	Beloved	Western

••••••••••••••••••••••••••••••••••

Fabayo	Lucky birth is joy	Nigeria
Faizah	Victorious	Northern
Fatia	One who conquers	Northern
Fatimah	Prophet's daughter	Northern
Fayola	Good fortune, honor	Nigeria

Feechi	Worship god	Western
Femi	Love me	Nigeria
Fola	Honor	Nigeria
Folade	Honor arrives	Western
Folami	Respect and honor me	Nigeria
Folashade	Honor confers crown	Nigeria
Folayan	She walks in dignity	Nigeria
Foluke	In god's care	Western
Fukayna	Knowledgeable, scholar	Northern
Fumiya	Suffering	Western
Fuvi	Born into suffering	Western
Fujo	Bringer of wholeness	Eastern

· ·

Ginikanwa	**Precious child**	**Western**
Gonza	Love	Uganda
Gulai	Born between rains	Eastern

· ·

Habiba	The beloved	**Eastern**
Habibka	Sweetheart	Western
Hadiah	Quiet and calm	Northern
Hadiya	Gift	Western
Hafsah	Wife of the prophet	Northern
Hagikah	Truthful	Northern
Halina	Gentle	Western
Hanifah	True believer	Northern
Haomyaro	Born during conflicts	Western
Hasina	She is good	Eastern
Hembadoon	The winner	Nigeria
Husniyah	Beautiful	Northern

. . . .

Idomenyin	Hope	Western
Idowu	First after twins	Nigeria
Ifama	Everything is fine	Nigeria
Ife	Lover of art	Western
Ifetayo	Love excels all	Nigeria
Ifma	Everything is fine	Nigeria
Ige	Delivered feet first	Nigeria
Iheoma	A welcome child	Western
Iheyinwa	by Divine Providence	Western
Ihuoma	Lucky, brings luck	Western
Ijeoma	A good journey	Western
Ijoma	Travel safely	Western
Ikuseghan	Peace surpasses war	Nigeria
Inaambura	Mother of the rains	Southern
Isoke	A gift from God	Nigeria
Ityiarmbiamo	I am against war	Nigeria
Iverem	Blessing and favor	Nigeria
Iyabo	Mother has returned	Nigeria
Izegbe	Long-expected child	Nigeria

. . . .

Jaha	Dignity	Western
Jamila	Beautiful	Western
Jendayi	Give thanks	Zimbabwe
Jendoyse	Good was done	Uganda
Jumoke	Everyone loves her	Western
Jwahir	Golden woman	Western

. . . .

Kabonero	Sign or omen	Uganda
Kadija	The prophet's wife	Western

Kafi	Serene	Central
Kagiso	Peace	Botswana
Kai	Lovable	Western
Kalifa	Holy child	Eastern
Kamania	The moon	Western
Kamba	Tortoise	Western
Karamoko	Studious	Western
Karimah	Generous	Northern
Katokwe	Happiness	Central
Kefilwe	I am given	Botswana
Kelinde	Second born of twins	Western
Kemba	Full of faith	Central
Kemuyetta	Beautiful music	Eastern
Kenyangi	White egret	Uganda
Kesi	Hard-working father	Eastern
Khatiti	Sweet little baby	Eastern
Khorsanhlai	She who brings sun	Western
Kibibi	Beautiful fat girl	Uganda
Kiho	Born on a foggy day	Uganda
Kijai	First girl born	Uganda
Kilolo	Shining youth	Central
Kisembo	A gift from God	Uganda
Kissa	Born after twins	Uganda
Komuntale	Born in lion country	Uganda
Komushana	Born in sunshine	Uganda
Kugonza	Love	Uganda
Kukoma	This one will not die	Nigeria
Kulabako	Quick look-a-pretty	Uganda
Kumiwa	Brave	Western
Kunto	Third child	Ghana
Kusmemererwa	Happiness	Uganda
Kwehangana	Endurance	Uganda

Africa

Day-of-the-Week and
Seasonal African names

In Africa, naming a girl after the day on which she was born is an especially popular custom. These day-of-the-week names, promininent in Ghana, run throughout the culture. Here are a few Ghanian examples:

Adwoa: born on Monday
Abena: born on Tuesday
Laraba: born on Wednesday
Aba: born on Thursday
Efua: born on Friday
Ama: born on Saturday
Esi: born on Sunday

Boys, too, are given day-of-the-week names. Examples include:

Coujoe: born on Monday
Coblah: born on Tuesday
Danjuma: born on Friday
Commie: born on Saturday
Danladi: born on Sunday

Names reflecting the season of birth are also frequent for both girls (Nafula meaning born during rains and Nagesa, born during harvest) and boys (Abegunde meaning born during holiday time; Abejide, born during winter; and Nadif, born between seasons).

● ●

Laraba	Wednesday	Western
Lateefah	Gentle, pleasant	Northern
Layia	Born at night	Western
Layla	Born at night	Eastern
Lebechi	Watch for God	Eastern
Limbe	Joyfulness	Western
Linda	Wait for goodness	Southern
Lindiwe	We waited for joy	Southern
Lololi	There is always love	Western
Lolonyo	Love is beautiful	Western
Lolovivi	Love is eternal	Western
Lozokun	Forget differences	Western
Lulu	A pearl, precious	Eastern
Lumengo	Flower of her people	Central

● ●

Magano	She is a gift	Southern
Maideyi	What did you expect?	Southern
Malene	Tower	Western
Manana	Lustrous	Western
Mandisa	Sweet	Southern
Mariama	Gift of god	Western
Marjani	Coral	Eastern
Marka	Steady rain	Western
Mashama	This is a surprise	Southern
Maudisa	Sweet	Western
Mawakana	I yield to ancestors	Southern
Mawiya	The essence of life	Northern
Mawusi	In the hands of God	Ghana
Migozo	Earnest	Southern
Mijiza	Works with her hands	Eastern

Moriba	Curious	Western
Morowa	Queen	Ghana
Mosi	First born child	Eastern
Mpho	Gift	Botswana
Mudiwa	Beloved	Western
Muga	Mother of all	Eastern
Mukarramma	Honored, respected	Northern
Mukumtagara	Born during wartime	Eastern
Muminah	Pious believer	Northern
Munirah	One who enlightens	Northern
Muslimah	Devout believer	Northern
Mwajuma	Born on Friday	Eastern
Mwamini	Honest	Eastern
Mwanahamisi	Born on Thursday	Eastern
Mwanajuma	Born on Friday	Eastern

· ·

Nabaasa	Omnipotent	Uganda
Nabinye	Producer of twins	Western
Nabossa	Sheep totem	Luganda
Nabukenya	Antelope totem	Luganda
Nabulungi	Beautiful one	Western
Nadia	Time of promise	Northern
Najat	Safe	Northern
Naeemah	Benevolent	Northern
Nafula	Born during rains	Western
Nagesa	Born during harvest	Uganda
Nailah	One who succeeds	Northern
Najuma	Abounding in joy	Eastern
Nakakande	Jungle	Luganda
Nakimera	A gift from God	Uganda
Nakpangi	This one is a star	Central
Nalo	Much loved	Western
Nalunga	A mushroom totem	Luganda

Nalungo	She is beautiful	Central
Namakula	Very pretty girl	Uganda
Namazzi	Water	Luganda
Nambogo	Buffalo clan	Uganda
Namirembe	Peace	Luganda
Namukasa	A goddess	Uganda
Nana	Mother of the earth	Western
Nangleni	Fish	Western
Nangoma	A princess	Luganda
Nankunda	Beloved	Uganda
Nantale	Lion clan totem	Uganda
Nanyamka	God's gift	Ghana
Nanziri	Fish clan totem	Uganda
Nataki	She is of royal birth	Central
Nathifa	Clean and pure	Northern
Nayo	We have joy	Western
Ndapewa	I was given this one	Southern
Ndunba	We are happy	Central
Ndunga	She will be famous	Central
Neema	Born in prosperity	Western
Neimat	Pleasant	Northern
Ngena	Majestic in service	Eastern
Ngina	One who serves	Eastern
Ngozi	Blessing	Western
Nini	Strong, industrious	Western
Njemile	Upstanding	Western
Njeri	Warrior's daughter	Eastern
Nkechi	Loyal	Western
Nkeka	Tenderness	Western
Nkenge	She is brilliant	Central
Nkosazana	Princess	Xhosa
Nne	Mother	Western
Nneke	Mother is prominent	Nigeria

Nnenia	Grandmother look-alike	Nigeria
Nobantu	Will be loved by all	Southern
Nobini	I now have two girls	Southern
Nobuhle	Beauty	Western
Nokhwezi	Morning star	Southern
Nomabaso	A welcomed present	Southern
Nomalanga	Sunny	Zulu
Nomatha	A real surprise	Southern
Nombeko	Respect	Xhosa
Nombese	Wonderful child	Western
Nomble	Beauty	Xhosa
Nombulelo	I give thanks	Southern
Nompumelelo	We have success	Southern
Nomsa	Kindness is found	Southern
Nomusa	This is mercy	Southern
Nondudumo	Born during thunder	Southern
Nondummiso	We give her praises	Southern
Nonggawuse	Send away falsehood	Southern
Noni	Gift of God	Western
Nonkululeko	Freedom is here	Southern
Nontando	Full of love	Southern
Nonthothuzelo	She will console us	Southern
Nonyameko	Patience	Western
Nonzwakazi	This is beauty	Southern
Noxolo	Peaceful	Southern
Nozibele	Generous one	Southern
Nsombi	Abounding joy	Central
Ntathu	I have three girls	Southern
Ntombentle	A lovely girl	Southern
Ntombizodwa	All are girls	Southern
Nun	Brightness	Northern
Nuru	Born in daylight	Eastern

Nwakaegbo	Worth more than money	Western
Nwanyiomaq	Beautiful lady	Western
Nwugo	Like an eagle	Western
Nyiramohoro	Peaceful	Western
Nzinga	Beauty and courage	Central

· ·

Oare	Saintly	Western
Obiagaeliaku	She comes to enjoy	Western
Obioma	Kindhearted	Western
Ode	Born along the road	Nigeria
Oji	Giftbearer	Western
Okola	Friendly	Western
Olabisi	Joy is multiplied	Nigeria
Olabunmi	Honor rewarded me	Nigeria
Olaniyi	Glory in wealth	Nigeria
Olubayo	Highest joy	Nigeria
Olubunmi	Highest gift	Nigeria
Olufemi	God loves me	Nigeria
Olufunka	Given to be loved	Nigeria
Olufunmilayo	God gives me joy	Nigeria
Oluremi	God consoles me	Nigeria
Omolara	Born at right time	Nigeria
Omorenomwara	Meant not to suffer	Nigeria
Omorose	My beautiful child	Nigeria
Oni	Desired	Nigeria
Oraefo	Affectionate	Western
Osayiomwabo	God will help us	Nigeria
Oseye	The happy one	Nigeria
Ozigbodi	Patience	Ghana
Ozioma	Good news	Western

• •

Panya	One of twins	Western
Pepukayi	We are awake	Southern
Pili	Second born	Eastern
Pumla	Now we can rest	Southern

• •

Qubilah	Concord	N. Africa

• •

Rabiah	Spring	Northern
Ramia	Prophet	Western
Ramla	Future predictor	Eastern
Raohiya	Agreeable	Western
Rasida	Righteous	Western
Raziya	Sweet and agreeable	Western
Rehema	Compassionate	Western
Rhamah	My sweetness	Eastern
Ripuree	Think about this	Southern
Rudo	Love	Southern
Rufano	Happiness	Western
Rufaro	Happiness	Southern
Rukiya	She rises on high	Eastern
Runako	Beauty	Southern

• •

Sabah	Morning	Northern
Sabiti	Born on Sunday	Uganda
Safiya	Clear-minded, pure	Eastern
Sagirah	Little one	Northern
Saidah	Happy, fortunate	Northern
Sakile	Peace and beauty	Southern
Sala	Gentle	Eastern

Salama	Peace	Eastern
Salihah	Correct, agreeable	Northern
Salma	Safe	Eastern
Sanyu	Happiness	Luganda
Sara	Gives pleasure	Northern
Sauda	Dark complexion	Eastern
Sekayi	Happy with laughter	Southern
Shaba	Morning has come	Northern
Shamfa	Sunshine	Eastern
Shami	Like the sun	Northern
Sharifa	Distinguished	Eastern
Shiminege	Sees the future	Nigeria
Sibongile	Thanks	Zimbabwe
Siboniso	Sign or omen	Zulu
Sigolwide	My ways are straight	Tanzania
Sihle	Beautiful	Southern
Sikhumbuzo	Reminder	Southern
Sikudhani	A surprise, unusual	Eastern
Sipo	A gift	Southern
Sit Abua	Her father loves her	Northern
Sit al-Banal	Master of girls	Northern
Sitembileq	Trust	Zimbabwe
Sithabile	We are happy	Southern
Siti	Lady	Eastern
Skukura	Grateful	Eastern
Soda	Happiness	Northern
Subira	Patience rewarded	Eastern
Syandene	Punctual	Tanzania

• •

Tabia	Talented	Eastern
Tahirah	Pure	Northern
Taiwo	First of twins	Yoruba
Talibah	Seeker of knowledge	Northern

Tatu	Third born	Eastern
Thandiwe	Loving one	Xhosa
Thema	Queen	Ghana
Themba	Trusted	Zulu
Thembeka	Trustworthy	Zulu
Thokozile	Happiness	Southern
Thuraia	Star of my life	Northern
Titilayo	Happiness is eternal	Nigeria
Torkwase	Queen	Nigeria
Tukesiga	Hopeful	Uganda
Tulimbwelu	We are in the light	Tanzania
Tulinagwe	God is with us	Tanzania
Tumpe	Let us thank God	Tanzania
Tumushabe	We pray to God	Uganda
Tumusiime	We thank God	Uganda
Tupokigwe	We are safe	Tanzania
Turyahumura	We will see God	Uganda
Tusuubira	We have hope	Uganda
Twaponilo	We are saved	Tanzania
Twesigye	We trust in God	Uganda
Twinamaani	We are powerful	Uganda

· ·

Uchefuna	My wits are about me	Nigeria
Umayma	Little mother	Northern
Umm	Mother	Northern
Urbi	Princess	Nigeria
Uvatera	God help us	Southern
Uwingabiye	Sent by the deity	Eastern

· ·

Vuyelwa	Joy	Southern
Vuyisa	Made happy	Southern

Nigerian Royalty Names

The letters "Ad" at the beginning of a name can mean connection to royalty. In a tribal culture, this is of utmost importance to establish the position of the child in the hierarchy of the community. It is also a source of family pride. Some examples of male royalty names are:

Adeagbo: He brings royal honor
Adebamgbe: Royalty dwells in me
Adedapo: Royalty unites the people
Adelaia: The crown settles quarrels
Ademola: He adds a crown to my wealth
Adegoke: The crown is exalted
Adetokunbo: Honor came from overseas
Adjua: Noble

A girl of noble birth might be named Adesimbo.

. . . .

| Wambui | Singer of songs | Eastern |
| Wesesa | Careless | Uganda |

. . . .

Yaa	Born on Thursday	Ghana
Yahimba	Nothing like home	Nigerian
Yaminah	Right and proper	Northern
Yejide	Her mother's image	Nigeria
Yetunde	Mother comes back	Nigeria

. . . .

Zahra	Flower	Tanzania
Zakiya	Intelligent	Eastern
Zalika	Well-born	Eastern
Zawadi	Gift	Eastern
Zesiro	Elder of twins	Uganda
Zenzele	She does it herself	Southern
Zine	I have four girls	Southern
Zihur	Flowers are plentiful	Northern
Zubaidah	Excellent	Northern
Zuwena	Good	Eastern

$\mathscr{A}$FRICA

Male

Name	Meaning	Region of Origin
Abanobi	There's no entrance to the mind	Western
Abaronye	Whom are you threatening?	Western
Abasi	Stern	Western
Abayomi	Born to bring joy	Nigeria
Abdu	Worshipper of God	Northern
Abdullah	Servant of God	Northern
Abdul-rahman	Servant of the merciful God	Northern
Abeeku	Born on Wednesday	Western
Abegunde	Born during holiday time	Nigeria
Abeid	A born leader	Eastern
Abejide	Born during winer	Nigeria
Abena	Pure	Western
Abi	To guard	Western
Abiade	Born of royal parents	Western
Abimbola	Born rich	Nigeria
Abiodun	Born at festival time	Nigeria
Abiola	Born at the New Year	Western
Abiona	Born during a journey	Nigeria
Abioye	Born at the time of coronation	Nigeria

Abosi	Life plant	Western
Abu	Nobility	Western
Abubakar	Noble	Western
Acholam	Do not provoke me	Western
Achufusi	Do not reject me	Western
Adama	Majestic	Western
Addae	Morning sun	Western
Ade	Of royal birth	Nigeria
Adeagbo	He brings royal honor	Nigeria
Adebamgbe	Royalty dwells in me	Nigeria
adebayo	Birth in a joyful time	Western
Adeboro	Royalty comes into wealth	Nigeria
Adedapo	Royalty unites the people	Nigeria
Adegoke	The crown is exalted	Nigeria
Adejola	The crown feeds on honor	Nigeria
Adelaja	The crown settles quarrels	Nigeria
Ademola	He adds a crown to my wealth	Western
Adesola	The crown has honored us	Nigeria
Adetokunbo	Honor came from overseas	Nigeria
Adewole	Royalty enters the house	Nigeria
Adeyemi	The crown suits me well	Nigeria
Adika	First born of second husband	Western

Adisa	One who makes himself clear	Western
Adjua	Noble	Western
Adofo	Warrior	Ghana
Adongo	First of twins	Uganda
Adroa	God's will	Luganda
Adunbi	Born to be pleasant	Nigeria
Afi	Spritual	Western
Afiba	By the sea	Western
Agu	Lion or leopard	Western
Agyei	Messenger from God	Ghana
Ahmed	Praiseworthy	Eastern
Ahoto	Peace	Western
Ahonya	Prosperity	Western
Ahurole	Loving	Western
Aiyetoro	Peace on earth	Western
Ajagbe	He carries off the prize	Nigeria
Ajamu	He fights for what he wants	Nigeria
Ajene	True	Western
Ajuluchukwu	Asked God for Child	Western
Akamafula	Work be rewarded	Western
Akia	First born	Uganda
Akiiki	Friend	Uganda
Akil	Intelligent, uses reason	Northern
Akin	A hero or strong man	Nigeria
Akinkawon	His bravery pacifies them	Nigeria
Akinlabi	We have a brave boy	Nigeria
Akinlana	Valor	Nigeria
Akinlawon	Bravery sustains them	Nigeria

Akinsanya	Valor avenges	Nigeria
Akinsheye	Valor acts honorably	Nigeria
Akinshiju	Valor awakes	Nigeria
Akintunde	A brave man has come	Western
Akinwole	Valor enters the house	Nigeria
Akinwunmi	Valor is pleasing to me	Nigeria
Ako	First born	Western
Akobundu	Prudence of life	Western
Akna	Born on Thursday	Western
Akua	Sweet messenger	Western
Akwete	Younger of twins	Western
Ali	Exhalted	N. Africa
Alimayu	God is honored	E. Africa
Ama	Happy	Western
Amaechi	Who knows the future?	Western
Amal	Hopes	Northern
Ambakisye	God is merciful to me	Western
Ambidwile	God has convinced me	Tanzania
Ambilikile	God called me	Tanzania
Ambokile	God has redeemed me	Tanzania
Ambonisye	God has rewarded me	Tanzania
Amin	Honest	Western
Aminata	Good character	Western
Amma	Famous	Western
Ampah	Trust is supreme	Western
Anàpa	Morning	Western

Andalwisye	God has shown me the way	Tanzania
Andengwisye	God has claimed me	Tanzaina
Angolwisye	God has guidied me	Tanzania
Angosisye	God sanctified me	Tanzania
Animashaun	Generous	Nigeria
Anjait	Born on grass	Uganda
Anwar	Shiny	N. Africa
Anyabwile	God has unchained me	Tanzania
Aondochimba	God is above all earth things	Nigeria
Apara	The child comes and goes	Nigeria
Aren	Eagle	Nigeria
Asukile	The lord has washed me	Tanzania
Atsu	Younger of twins	Ghana
Ato	This one is brilliant	E. Africa
Atuanya	Son born, expected daughter	Nigeria
Ayele	Powerful	E. Africa
Ayinde	We praised and he came	Nigeria
Ayo	Happiness	Nigeria
Ayodele	Joy enters this house	Nigeria
Ayzize	Let it come	S. Africa
Azagba	Born out of town	Nigeria
Azi	Energy of youth	Nigeria
Azibo	Earth	Malawi
Azikiwe	Vigorous	Nigeria

Nigerian Holy Names

An individual's "chi" (compare to the Chinese chi [vital energy]) is considered of utmost importance. In the Nigerian tradition, a person's chi is thought to be a personal god that comes into life with the child and follows the individual throughout life. This is similar to the Christian concept of a guardian angel, except that chi can cause misfortune as well as good fortune. Many names beginning with Chi relate to this concept of deity.

Examples of female Chi names:

Chinasaokuru: God answers for me
Chinue: God's blessing
Chioneso: Guiding light
Chizoba: Protected (by God)

Examples of male Chi names:

Chijioke: God gives talent
Chike: Power of God
Chinelo: Thought of God
Chioke: Gift to God

• •

Babatunde	Image of grand-father	Nigeria
Babatunji	Another image of grandfather	Nigeria
Babru	Born at the full moon	Tanzania
Babu	Doctor	E. Africa
Badrak	He has mercy	Northern
Bahari	One who sails	Northern
Bahemuka	Resembles his father	Uganda
Bakari	Of noble promise	E. Africa
Balinda	Fortitude, patience, endurance	Uganda
Balogun	Warlord	Nigeria
Balondemu	Chosen one	Uganda
Bandele	Born away from home	Nigeria
Banga	Sharp as a knife	S. Africa
Banjoki	Stay with me and go no more	Nigeria
Baruti	Teacher	Gotswana
Basel	Bravery is his prize	Northern
Becktemba	Trusted	Zimbabwe
Beesigye	Trust in God	Uganda
Begumisa	Indefatigable	Uganda
Bem	Peace	Nigeria
Betserai	Sent as a helper	Zimbabwe
Bhoke	Wanderer	E. Africa
Bilal	First convert of the prophet	Northern
Birungi	Nice, pretty, perfect	Luganda
Bobo	Born on Tuesday	Ghana
Bomani	Warrior	Malawi

Bongani	Sing with joy	Zimbabwe
Boseda	Born on Sunday	Nigeria
Bwagilo	Source of all things	Tanzania
Bwana Mkubwa	Great master	E. Africa
Bwerani	You are welcome	Malawi
Bwire	Born at night	Uganda
Byaitaka	Born to die	Uganda
Byarugaba	For, by, or of God	Uganda
Byembandwa	Named for a god	Uganda

· ·

Chabwere	He has arrived	Malawi
Chafulumisa	Swift	Malawi
Chatha	An ending	Malawi
Chatuluka	A departure	Malawi
Chenzira	Born during a journey	Zimbabwe
Chibale	Kindship	Malawi
Chigaru	Hound	Malawi
Chijioke	God gives talent	Nigeria
Chike	Power of God	Nigeria
Chinelo	Thought of God	Nigeria
Chinua	God's blessing	Nigeria
Chioke	Gift to God	Nigeria
Chionesu	Guiding light	Zimbabwe
Chiumbo	Small creation	Kenya
Chuma	Wealth, beads	Zimbabwe
Coblah	Born on Tuesday	Ghana
Coffie	Born on Friday	Ghana
Commie	Born on Saturday	Ghana
Coujoe	Born on Monday	Ghana

· ·

| Dada | Curly-haired boy | Nigeria |

Dakarai	Happiness	Zimbabwe
Damani	Thoughtful	Western
Danjuma	Born on Friday	Western
Danladi	Born on Sunday	Western
Darweshi	Saintly	Eastern
Daudi	Beloved	Eastern
Dawud	Beloved	Northern
Dia	Champion	Western
Diallo	Bold	Western
Diarra	Gift	Western
Dibia	Healer	Western
Diji	Farmer	Western
Dike	Brave warrior	Western
Diliza	Destroyer of evil	Southern
Dingane	He comes in time of need	Southern
Diop	Ruler, scholar	Central
Djenaba	Affectionate	Western
Donkor	Humble	Ghana
Duguma	Sharp as a spear	Western
Dukuzumurenyi	Praise to God	Western
Dumisani	Herald of the future	Southern
Dunduza	Adventurous	Central
Durojaiye	Enjoyment	Nigeria
Duruji	Farmer	Western

• •

Ebo	Born on Tuesday	Ghana
Eberechukwu	God's mercy	Western
Ede	Sweetness	Western
Edo	Love	Western
Ehioze	Above jealousy	Nigera
Eintou	Pearl	Western
Ejau	We have received	Uganda

Ejiikeme	Do not use force	Western
Ekeama	Nature is splendid	Western
Ekechukwu	God's creation	Western
Ekundayo	Sorrow turns to happiness	Western
Ekwutosi	Speak not against others	Western
El Fatih	The conqueror	Northern
Emenike	Do not use force	Western
Enobakhare	The king's word	Nigeria
Enomwoyi	Graceful and charming	Western
Erasto	A man of peace	Northern
Ewansiha	Secrets are not for sale	Nigeria
Eze	King	Western
Ezeamaka	The King is splendid	Western
Ezenachi	The king rules	Western
Ezeoha	The people's king	Western

• •

Fadahunsi	Royalty has favored me	Northern
Fadil	Generous	Northern
Fakih	One who recites the Koran	Northern
Fanta	Beautiful day	Western
Faraji	Consolation	Eastern
Farri	A religious man	Northern
Fati	Robust	Western
Fatou Mata	Beloved by all	Western
Febechi	Worshiper of God	Western
Femi	Beloved	Western
Fenuku	Born after twins	Western

Fenyang	Conqueror	Botswana
Foluke	He is in God's hands	Nigeria
Fouad	Heart	Northern
Fudail	Excellent character	Northern
Fulumirani	A journey	Malawi
Funsani	Request	Malawi

Gaika	Gifted in sculpture	Southern
Galabba	Talker	Uganda
Gamba	Warrior	Zimbabwe
Garai	Be settled	Rhodesia
Gavivi	Money is good	Western
Ginikanwa	A valuable child	Western
Goatsemondime	God knows	Botswana
Gogo	Looks like grandfather	Nguni
Gonza	Love	Uganda
Goredenna	Black cloud	Zimbabwe
Gowan	Rainmaker	Nigeria
Gyasi	Wonderful	Ghana

Habib	Beloved	Northern
Hamadi	Praised	Eastern
Hamidi	Commendable	Eastern
Hamisi	Born on Thursday	Eastern
Hamza	Historically significant person	Northern
Hanbal	Purity	Northern
Hanif	True believer	Northern
Harb	Warrior	Northern
Harith	Cultivator	Northern
Hasani	Handsome	Eastern

Hashim	Crusher of evil	Northern
Hondo	Warrior	Zimbabwe

. . . .

Idi	Born during the Idi festival	Eastern
Iimarogve	Born to a good family	Nigeria
Irunba	Born following twins	Uganda
Isabirye	He fathers twins	Uganda
Ishag	He laughed when he was born	Northern
Isingoma	First of twins	Uganda
Issa	God is our slavation	Eastern
Iyapo	Many trails	Nigeria

. . . .

Jabari	Brave	Eastern
Jabulani	Be happy	Zimbabwe
Jahi	Dignity	Eastern
Jaja	Honored	Nigeria
Jamal	Beauty	Northern
Jaramogi	Traveller	Eastern
Jawanza	Dependable	Central
Jawhar	Jewel essence	Northern
Jelani	Mighty	Eastern
Jibade	Born close to royalty	Nigeria
Jibri	Archangel of Allah	Northern
Jimiyu	Born in the dry season	Uganda
Jojo	A storyteller	Eastern
Jongilanga	He faces the sun	Southern
Juma	Born on Friday	Eastern
Jumanne	Born on Tuesday	Eastern

Jumoke	Everyone loves him	Nigeria

· ·

Kabiito	**B**orn when foreigners visiting	Uganda
Kabonero	Sign or omen	Uganda
Kabonesa	Birth caused lots of trouble	Uganda
Kacancu	First born son	Uganda
Kafele	Worth dying for	Malawi
Kakuyon	He arms the people	Central
Kakyomya	Ancient Banyoro god	Uganda
Kalonji	He will be victorious	Central
Kamau	Quite warrior	Kenya
Kambui	Fearless	Eastern
Kamdibe	Let me endure	Western
Kampihe	Go and see	Western
Kamukama	Protected by God	Uganda
Kaozi	Mountain	Uganda
Karanja	A guide	Central
Kareem	Generous	Northern
Karume	Protector of land and forest	Central
Kashka	Friendly	Western
Kasimu	Keeper of the forest	Western
Kasiya	Departure	Western
Katungi	Rich person	Uganda
Kayin	Long hoped-for child	Nigeria
Kayode	He brought joy	Western
Kayonga	Great warrior of Ankole clan	Uganda
Kazandu	You are a young man	Southern
Keambiroiro	Mountain of blackness	Kenya

Keanjaho	Mountain of beans	Kenya
Kefentse	Conqueror	Botswana
Keita	Worshipper	Western
Kelechi	Thanks be to God	Western
Kenyatta	A musician	Central
Kereenyaga	Mountain of mystery (Mt. Kenya)	Kenya
Ketema	He comes from the valley	Central
Khalfani	Destined to rule	Eastern
Khalid	Eternal	Northern
Khari	Kingly	Western
Kiambu	He will be rich	Central
Kibuuka	Brave Buganda warrior	Uganda
Kimani	Sailor	Eastern
Kiho	Born on a foggy day	Uganda
Kiintu	Man who first came to Buganda	Uganda
Kitwana	Pledged to live	Eastern
Kizza	Born after twins	Luganda
Kodwo	Born on Monday	Ghana
Kofi	Born on Friday	Ghana
Kogongo	Born before twins	Luganda
Kojo	Unconquerable	Ghana
Konata	Man of high station	Western
Kokayi	Summon the people	Eastern
Kondo	Warrior	Eastern
Kondwani	Joyful	Malawi
Kontor	Only child	Ghana
Kopano	Union	Tswana
Kpodo	Elder of twins	Ghana
Kudyauku	Feast	Malawi
Kugonza	Love	Uganda

Kunle	Home filled with honors	Nigeria
Kwacha	Morning	Malawi
Kwada	Night has fallen	Malawi
Kwakou	Born on Wednesday	Ghana
Kwayera	Dawn	Malawi
Kwesi	Conquering strength	Western

• •

Landuleni	One who finds greatness	Southern
Langalibaele	Sunshine	Southern
Lasana	A poet of the people	Central
Lateef	Gentle, pleasant	Northern
Leabua	You speak	Southern
Ligongo	Who is this?	Western
Lisimba	Lion	Malawi
Lizwelicha	New world	Zimbabwe
Liu	Voice	Malawi
Lotachukwu	Remember God	Western
Lukman	Prophet	Northern
Lumumba	Gifted, brilliant	Central
Lutalo	Warrior	Luganda
Luzige	Locust	Uganda

• •

Madzimoyo	Water of life	Malawi
Mahuli	He is a victor	Southern
Makonnen	Ruler	Eastern
Makutano	Born in a meeting place	Western
Makwangwala	Crown	Malawi
Malawa	Flowers	Malawi
Malek	Owner	Northern

Mamoun	Confident	Northern
Mangwiro	The enlightened one	Southern
Mani	He comes from the mountain	Central
Mapfumo	The soldier	Southern
Marwan	Historical personage	Northern
Masomakali	Sharp eyes	Tanzania
Masud	Fortunate	Eastern
Mawali	There is a God	Western
Mawulawde	God will provide	Ghana
Mawulode	God will provide	Western
Mayanga	A sailor of lakes	Luganda
Mlengalenga	Heaven	Malawi
Mbabazi	Mercy	Uganda
Mbita	Born on a cold night	Eastern
Mbonisi	One who will teach us	Southern
Mbwana	Master	Eastern
Mbwelera	Return	Malawi
Mbyiu	Fast runner	Eastern
Mganga	Doctor	Eastern
Mhina	Delightful	Eastern
Minkah	Justice	Ghana
Mirembe	Peace	Luganda
Mlengalenga	Heaven	Malawi
Moderia	Teacher	Western
Modibo	Helper	Western
Mombera	Adventurous	Eastern
Mongo	Famous	Nigeria
Mohammed	Thankful	Northern
Molefi	He keeps traditions	Southern
Mosi	First born	Tanzania
Moswen	Light in color	Botswana
Moyenda	Born on a journey	Malawi

Moyo	Health and well-being	Malawi
Mpagi	Pillar of the community	Uganda
Mposi	Blacksmith	Tanzania
Mpumelele	Success	Zulu
Mpyama	He shall inherit	Central
Mthuthuzeli	Comforter	Xhosa
Mtima	Heart	Malawi
Mtumwa	Pledged	Eastern
Mtundu	Community of people	Malawi
Mudada	Provider	Zimbabwe
Muga	Given by God	Uganda
Mugabe	Intelligent, quick	Central
Mugeta	Born at night	Eastern
Mugisa	Lucky	Uganda
Muhammad	Praised	Eastern
Muhindo	First-born son	Uganda
Muhoozi	Revenges wrongs	Uganda
Muhumuza	Brings peace and calm	Uganda
Mukasa	Chief administrator	Uganda
Mukisa	Good luck	Luganda
Mulindwa	He is protected	Uganda
Mulogo	Wizard	Uganda
Mulumba	One who attacks	Luganda
Musa	Sharp	Northern
Musaazi	A joker	Uganda
Musabingo	Savior	Uganda
Musembwa	Monkey clan	Uganda
Muslim	Believer	Northern
Musoke	Born under a rainbow	Uganda

Mutope	Protector	Central
Mvula	Rain	Malawi
Mwai	Good fortune	Malawi
Mwaka	Born on New Year's Eve	Uganda
Mwamba	Strong	Tanzania
Mwando	An efficient worker	Eastern
Mwangi	He will have many children	Eastern
Mwanje	Leopard	Luganda
Mwendapole	He takes his time	Tanzania
Mwesige	Trust	Uganda
Mwinyi	King	Eastern
Mwita	The summoner	Eastern

· ·

Nabate	Little one	Western
Nadif	Born between seasons	Eastern
Nadir	Rare	Northern
Naeem	Benevolent	Northern
Nangila	Born during a journey	Uganda
Nantambu	Man of destiny	Western
Nassor	Victorious	Tanzania
Nazim	Wonderful	Northern
Ndabeexinhle	This is good news	Southern
Ndoro	A shell (emblem of kingship)	Southern
Ndubia	May life come	Western
Ngozi	Blessing	Nigeria
Ngugi	The traditions are set	Eastern
Nikusubila	Hopeful	Tanzania

Nizam	Discipliner, arranger	Northern
Njabulo	Happiness	Southern
Njonjo	Disciplined	Eastern
Nkokheli	Leader	Southern
Nkosi	Ruler	Zulu
Nkpume	Solid as rock	Western
Nkululeko	Freedom is ours	Southern
Nnabugwu	Father is honor	Western
Nnaemeka	Father has done much	Western
N'Namdi	Father's name lives on	Nigeria
N'Nanna	Grandfather's name lives on	Nigeria
Nogomo	He will be prosperous	Central
Nuru	Born in daylight	Eastern
Nwabudike	Son is the father's power	Nigeria
Nyahuma	A helper of others	Central
Nyandoro	He wears the crown	Southern
Nyenyedzi	Star	Southern
Nyikadzino	This land belongs to us	Southern
Nyatui	Tiger fighter	Uganda

· ·

Oba	**King**	**Western**
Obadele	The king comes home	Western
Obiajulu	The heart is consoled	Western
Obinna	Dear to the father	Western
Obinwoke	Manly heart	Western

Ochi	Laughter	Western
Odinakachukwu	In God's hands	Western
Oding	An artist	Eastern
Ogbo	Companion	Western
Ogbonna	Image of his father	Nigeria
Oginga	One who drums	Eastern
Ogwanbi	Fortunate	Western
Oidu	Sharp-eyed	Uganda
Ojemba	Traveller	Western
Ojore	Man of war	Uganda
Okechukwu	God's gift	Nigeria
Okello	Born after twins	Uganda
Okoth	Born during a rainstorm	Uganda
Okware	Born at night	Uganda
Okwayi	God	Uganda
Ola	Wealth	Nigeria
Olabisi	Joy is multiplied	Western
Olamina	This is my wealth	Western
Olaniyan	Honors surround me	Nigeria
Olu	Preeminent	Western
Olubayo	Greatest joy	Western
Olufemi	God loves me	Western
Olugbala	Savior of the people	Nigeria
Olukayode	My lord brings happiness	Nigeria
Olumide	My lord arrives	Nigeria
Olusola	God has blessed me	Western
Omar	Trustworthy	Northern
Omorede	Prince	Western
Onuchukwu	God's voice	Western
Onyait	Born on grass	Uganda
Onyango	Born in the morning	Uganda
Oronde	Appointed	Central

Orunjan	Midday sun	Nigeria
Osagboro	There is only one god	Western
Osagie	God agrees	Western
Osayaba	God forgives	Western
Othiamba	Born in the afternoon	Uganda
Othieno	Born at night	Uganda
Owodunni	It's nice to have money	Nigeria

. . . .

Paki	Witness	Western
Patire	Where we are	Western
Pili	Second born	Western

. . . .

Rami	He is wise	Northern
Rapuluchukwu	Leave it in God's hands	Western
Rapuokwu	Abstain from quarrels	Western
Rasidi	Good council	Western
Rikondja	Our nation is struggling	Southern
Rwakaikara	God of the Banyoro people	Uganda
Rudo	Love	Zimbabwe
Runako	Handsome	Zimbabwe

. . . .

Sabiti	Born on Sunday	Uganda
Sadiki	Faithful	Uganda
Saeed	Happy, fortunate	Northern

Safe el-din	Sword of the religion	Northern
Salah	Good is a reward	Northern
Salim	Peace	Northern
Salih	Good, right, proper	Northern
Sanga	He came from the valley	Central
Sanyu	Happiness	Luganda
Sekou	Fighter	Western
Sekpuluchi	Praise God	Western
Sempala	Born in a prosperous time	Uganda
Sentwaki	Courageous	Eastern
Senyange	White egret	Luganda
Sera	Goddess in Lugisu tradition	Uganda
Setimba	Named after river Setimba	Uganda
Shakir	Thankful	Northern
Shawki	Yearning for right conduct	Northern
Shermarke	Bringer of good fortune	Western
Shomari	Forceful	Eastern
Shuaib	Qur'anic prophet	Northern
Shumba	Lion	Southern
Sigidi	He is like a thousand	Southern
Sikukkun	Born on Christmas Day	Western
Sikumbuzo	The ancestors remind us	Southern
Simangaliso	He came quickly	Southern
Simba	Strength of a lion	Southern

Simwenyi	One who smiles all the time	Western
Sipho	A gift	Southern
Siyolo	This is joy	Southern
Sokoni	He came from the sea	Central
Solwazi	He is knowledge	Southern
Sowande	Wise healer	Nigeria
Sudi	Luck	Eastern
Suhuba	Friend	Tanzania
Sulaiman	Peaceful	Northern
Sule	Adventurous	Western
Sultan	Ruler	Eastern

• •

Taamiti	Bravery	Uganda
Tabansi	Endure patiently	Western
Tacuma	He is alert	Central
Tageni	Let us give praise	Southern
Tagulani	Be happy	Southern
Taiwo	First born of twins	Western
Tapfuma	We are wealthy	Southern
Tayebwsa	God never forgets	Uganda
Tegogo	Gratitude	Western
Thabiti	A true man	Kenya
Thair	Honest and clean	Northern
Thambo	Ground	Western
Tibyangye	Everything belongs to God	Uganda
Tobechukwu	Praise God	Western
Toola	Workman	Western
Tor	King	Nigeria
Tukesiga	Hopeful	Uganda
Tumaini	Hope	Kenya
Tumushabe	We pray to God	Uganda

Tumusiime	We thank God	Uganda
Tusuubira	We have hope	Uganda
Twesigye	Let's trust in God	Uganda
Twinamaani	We are powerful	Uganda
Tyehimba	We stand as a nation	Nigeria

· ·

Ubaid	Faithful	Northern
Uche	Thought	Nigeria
Uthman	Companion of the Prophet	Northern

· ·

Vuai	Savior	Eastern

· ·

Wafor	Born on Afor market day	Nigeria
Walialu	He makes things return	Eastern
Wamukota	Left-handed	Uganda
Wamusa	Never satisfied with his wealth	Western
Weke	Born on Eke market day	Western
Wimana	He belongs to the deity	Eastern

· ·

Yafeu	Bold	Ghana
Yahya	God's gift	Eastern
Yakubu	He is blessed	Northern
Yamro	Courteous	Central
Yao	Born on Thursday	Western

Yazid	Ever increasing	Northern
Yero	A born soldier	Central
Yerodin	Studious	Central
Yobachi	Pray to God	Western
Yohance	God's gift	Nigeria
Yusef	The promise is true	Northern
Yusuf	He shall add to his powers	Eastern

• •

Zahur	Flower	Eastern
Zaid	Increase, growth	Northern
Zesireo	Elder of twins	Western
Zuberi	Strong	Eastern

African Order-of-Birth Names

In Uganda, as in many other African countries, a child is often named in the birth order. (Compare to the Oriental tradition of Elder brother, or Youngest sister.) Sometimes these particular identifying names are added later, such as born before twins. Twins are often part of African names as shown below.

Examples of female order-or-birth names:

> Babirye: First of twins
> Doto: Second of twins
> Ekellot: Girl after twins
> Kijai: First girl born
> Kissa: Born after twins
> Tatu: Third born

Examples of male order-of-birth names:

> Akia: First born
> Akwete: Younger of twins
> Fenuku: Born after twins
> Isingoma: First of twins
> Muhindo: First-born son
> Okello: Born after twins

ARABIC (ISLAMIC) NAMES

Arabic and Moslem names have not undergone the seachanges that Christian and European names have experienced. Since the time of the Prophet— nearly two thousand years ago—they have remained unchanged.

Because of this enduring stability, these names have penetrated many cultures. For example, a high percentage of Swahili names are readily recognized as variants of Arabic originals.

Far-ranging traders, Arabs were active in the spice and slave-trade, leaving their imprint wherever they went.

Many Arabic names are derived from the 99 names, or attributes, of Allah.

Other popular Moslem names refer to the Prophet. With more than 500 variations available, there is plenty from which to choose! A pious Moslem saying is "If you have a hundred sons, name them all Muhammad." Other choices include the names of the Prophet's wives and family.

In addition to names of religious significance, Arabic names often claim a quality or virtue, which parents hope their child will acquire in life. Some examples of girl's names are: Adeeba, literary woman; Alia, lofty; Farzaana, intelligent; and Qaderra, competent. Boy's names include: 'Aabid, worshipper; Dalair, valiant; Faarooq, distinguished; and Iman, faithful.

Nature names — flowers, atmospheric references, animals — are also used. A girl, for example, could be called Rabiah, breeze, and her brother might be Numair, panther.

Since Arabs consider it extremely rude to have a person's name used commonly, prefixes are often attached to give the name a distinctive characteristic. Abu means father of; Um, mother of; Bin and Binte, daughter of; and Ibn, son of. Thus the father of Zarifa (graceful) would be Abu Zarifa and her mother could be called Um Zarifa, in addition to the parent's own personal name. Each differentiation is added during one's lifetime, so that a person's name can become quite long. Children might substitute bint (daughter of) or ibn (son of) with their parent's name in place of their own name and be called, for example, bint Salamah (daughter of Salamah) or ibn Asad (son of Asad).

It is also incumbent upon Moslems to choose names with goodly meanings, not denoting any evil.

The 99
Glorious Names of Allah

Name	Meaning
Adh-Dhaarr	The Afflicter
Al-'Adil	The Justice
Al-'Afuw	The Effacer
Al-Ahad	The Unique
Al-'Aleem	The Omniscient
Al-'Ali	The Most High
Al-'Azeem	The Mighty
Al-'Azeez	The Almighty
Al-Aakhir	The Last
Al-Awwal	The First
Al-Baa'ith	The Resurrector
Al-Baaqee	The Everlasting
Al-Baaree	The Artificer
Al-Baasit	The Expander
Al-Baatin	The Interior
Al-Badee'	The Wonderful
Al-Bar	The Pious
Al-Baseer	The Discerning
Al-Fattaah	The Revealer
Al-Ghaffaar	The Forgiver
Al-Ghafoor	The Pardoner
Al-Ghanee	The All Sufficing
Al-Haadee	The Guide

Name	Meaning
Al-Hafeez	The Guardian
Al-Hai'yy	The Alive
Al-Hakam	The Judge
Name	Meaning
Al-Hakeem	The Judicious
Al-Haleem	The Clement
Al-Hameed	The Praiseworthy
Al-Haseeb	The Noble
Al-Huqq	The Truth
Al-Jaami'	The Comprehensive
Al-Jabbaar	The All Compelling
Al-Jaleel	The Honorable
Al-Kabeer	The Great
Al-Kareem	The Bountiful
Al-Khaafidh	The Humbler
Al-Khaaliq	The Creator
Al-Khabeer	The Aware One
Al-Lateef	The Gracious
Al-Maajid	The Illustrious
Al-Maani'	The Prohibiter
Al-Majeed	The Glorious
Al-Malik	The King
Al-Mateen	The Strong
Al-Mu'akhkhir	The Fulfiller
Al-Mu'eed	The Restorer
Al-Mu'izz	The Exhalter
Al-Mu'min	The Faithful
Al-Mubdee	The Creator
Al-Mughnee	The Bestower
Al-Muhaimin	The Vigilant
Al-Muhsee	The Accountant
Al-Muhyee	The Life Giver

Name	Meaning
Al-Mujeeb	The Respondent
Al-Mumeet	The Bringer of Death
Al-Muntaqim	The Avenger
Al-Muqaddim	The Advancer
Name	Meaning
Al-Muqeet	The Nourisher
Al-Muqsit	The Just
Al-Muqtadir	The All Powerful
Al-Musawwir	The Designer
Al-Mut'all	The Most High
Al-Mutakabbir	The Majestic
Al-Muzill	The Subduer
Al-Qaabidh	The Recipient
Al-Qaadir	The Omnipotent
Al-Qawwee	The Powerful
Al-Qayyoom	The Eternal
Al-Quahhaar	The Dominant
Al-Quddoos	The Holy One
Al-Waahid	The Holy One
Al-Waajid	The Opulent
Al-Waalee	The Master
Al-Waarith	The Inheritor
Al-Waasi'	The Omnipresent
Al-Wadood	The Loving
Al-Wahhaab	The Donor
Al-Wakeel	The Guardian
Al-Walee	The Defender
An-Naafi'	The Beneficial
An-Noor	The Light
Ar-Ra'oof	The Merciful
Ar-Raafi'	The Exhalter
Ar-Raheem	The Most Compassionate

Name	Meaning
Ar-Rahman	The Most Merciful
Ar-Raqeeb	The Watchful
Ar-Rasheed	The Guide
Ar-Razzaaq	The Sustainer
As-Saboor	The Enduring
Name	Meaning
As-Salaam	The Tranquillity
As-Samad	The Perfect
As-Samee'	The All Hearing
Ash-Shaheed	The Witness
Ash-Shakoor	The Grateful
At-Tawaab	The Relenting
Az-Zaahir	The Apparent
Wal Ikraam	Lord of Majesty
Zul-Jalaal	Lord of Splendid Glory

ARABIC

Female

Name	Meaning
Aamina	Secured, protected
Aamira	Royal, rich
Aaquila	Rational, intelligent
Aaraa	Embellishing, adorning
Aarifa	Knowing, aware of
'Abieda	Worshipper
Adeeba	Literary woman
'Afa'f	Chastity
Akilah	Logical
Alea	Exhalted
Aleah	Variation of Alea
'Aleema	Learned
Alhena	Ring
Alia	Lofty
Alima	Sea maiden
Almaas	Diamond
Almira	Princess
Alzubra	Name of a star in Leo
Ameena	Trustworthy
Ameera	Princess
Amina	Secure
Aminah	Variation of Amina
Amineh	Faithful
Aneesa	Afffectionate
Anjum	Stars
Asha	From Ayasha, life

Ashia	Life
'Atiyya	Gift
Ayasha	Life
'Azza	To be mighty
'Azeeza	Respected

· ·

Baano	Lady
Bahaar	Spring
Baqia	Jewel
Barika	Bloom, or success
Basheera	Glad tidings
Basimah	Smiling
Batool	Virgin
Bibi	Lady
Bilquees	Queen of Sheba
Bushraa	Good news

· ·

Chardae	Runaway
Charde	Variation of Chardae

· ·

Dayana	Divine

· ·

Emmali	Industrious

· ·

Faakhira	Magnificent
Faatin	Charming
Fadhaahat	Elegant
Fadheelat	Virtue

Fahmeeda	Wise
Faiza	Victorious
Faraana	Happy
Faraasat	Perceptive
Faraaz	Ascent to the heights
Farah	Joy
Fareeda	Unique
Farhat	Delight
Farkhanda	Fortunate
Farzaana	Intelligent
Fatima	Daughter of the Prophet
Fatma	Variation of Fatima
Fatmeh	Variation of Fatima
Firdaus	Garden of Paradise
Firdausee	Heavenly

• •

Gauhar	**Pearl**
Genna	Small bird
Ghadah	Young, fresh, tender
Gulshan	Rose

• •

Haajiraq	**Migrant**
Habeeba	Sweetheart
Habibah	Beloved
Hafeesa	Keeper
Haidera	Lioness
Halima	Generous
Hameeda	Glorious
Hanaa'	Bliss
Haneefa	True
Haseena	Beautifully

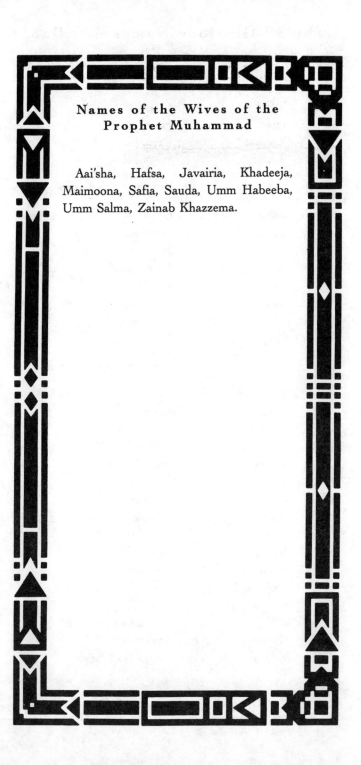

Names of the Wives of the Prophet Muhammad

Aai'sha, Hafsa, Javairia, Khadeeja, Maimoona, Safia, Sauda, Umm Habeeba, Umm Salma, Zainab Khazzema.

• •

'Iffat	Chastity
Iman	Faith
'Inaayat	Favored
'Ishrat	Pleasurable

• •

Jalila	Great
Jamell	Good-looking
Jamil	Handsome
Jamila	From Jamil
Jamilah	Beautiful
Jannat	Garden
Jarita	Earthen water jug
Jessenia	Flower

• •

Kabeera	Great
Kaela	Sweetheart
Kaelyn	Form of Kaela
Kailey	Variation of Kaela
Kaleela	From Kalila
Kaleema	Speaker
Kalila	Girlfriend
Kalilla	Variation of Kalila
Kalyn	Variation of Kalila
Kamila	Perfect
Kamilah	Variation of Kamila
Kamillah	Variation of Kamila
Kareema	Precious
Karida	Untouched, virginal
Kaylene	Sweetheart
Kayley	Variation of Kaylene

Kaylil	Variation of Kaylene
Kaylin	From Kalila
Khaalida	Immortal
Khaanam	Lady
Khaatoonq	Noble woman
Khadijah	Trustworthy
Kubraa	Senior woman

. . . .

La'eeqa	Elegant
Lailaa	Night
Latavia	Pleasant
Lateefa	Jest
Lilith	Of the night
Lubnaq	Mouthful

. . . .

Maajida	Glorious
Ma'asooma	Impeccable
Ma'azza	Respectful
Mahbooba	Beloved
Mahmooda	Praiseworthy
Maimouna	Trustworthy
Majeeda	Respectful
Malika	Queen
Mamtaz	Distinguished
Mariyah	Sea child
Maryam	Wished-for child
Mas'ooda	Lucky
Medina	City (place name)
Meenaa	Star
Mubaarika	Blessed
Mu'mina	Faithful
Muneera	Brilliant

Muqaddisa	Holy
Musarrat	Delight
Musawwira	Artist

. . . .

Naadia	Runner
Naadira	Rare
Naaheed	Morning star
Naa'ila	Winner
Naasira	Helper
Naazeen	Delicate
Naazima	Poet
Nabeela	Noble
Nadira	Rare
Na'eema	Joyful
Nafessa	Precious
Naghma	Melody
Najeeba	Star
Naqeeba	Soul
Nargis	Narcissus
Naseebaq	Fortune
Naseem	Gentle breeze
Nasreen	Jonquil
Nazaakat	Neat
Neelam	Blue gem
Neelofar	Lotus
Nepa	Walking backwards
Nisaa'	Womanly
Noura	Light
Numa	Delight
Nuzhat	Freshness

. . . .

Qadeera	Competent

Qaisera	Empress
Qamar	Moon
Qiturah	Tranquil
Qudsiyya	Holy

· ·

Ra'anaa	Graceful
Raanee	Queen
Raashida	Conscious
Rabiah	Breeze
Raessa	Matron
Raf'at	Of high rank
Rafee'a	Elevated
Rafeeqa	Companion
Raheema	Beneficient
Rahmah	Mercy
Rasheeda	Pious
Rehaana	Fragrant
Rida	In God's favor
Rihana	Sweet basil
Roohee	Spiritual
Ruby	Precious
Ruqayyah	Superior (daughter of the Prophet)

· ·

Saabaah	Morning
Saabira	Patient
Sa'adia	Fortunate
Saadiqa	Truthful
Saahira	Magician
Saa'iqa	Lightening
Saajida	Adorer
Saaleha	Virtuous
Sabaah	Dawn

Sabeeha	Beautiful
Sa'eeda	Lucky
Sahar	Enchanting
Sakeena	Tranquil
Salama	Peaceful
Saleema	Mild
Salwaa	Quail
Sameean	Jovial
Sameh	One who forgives
Sana	Radiance
Sanobar	Pine tree
Sayyeda	Lady
Seemeen	Silver
Shaahida	Beloved
Shaa'ista	Polite
Shaakira	Thankful
Shafeeqa	Compassionate
Shagufta	Flourishing
Shahar	By the moon
Shahzaade	Princess
Shakeela	Well-shaped
Shamarra	Prepare for battle
Shatara	Industrious
Sheereen	Pleasant
Sherika	Easterner
Siddiqa	Friend
Sultana	Empress
Syreeta	Companion

· ·

Taahira	Pure
Taaj	Crown
Taara	Star
Tabassam	Smiling

Tahiyya	Greeting
Takia	Worshiper
Taliba	Student
Taskeen	Peaceful
Tasneem	Fountain of paradise
Taufeeqa	Prosperous
Tayyaba	Chaste
Thameena	Valuable
Tharwat	Powerful
Thorayya	Star of the Pleiades
Tohfa	Uncommon

• •

Um Kolthum	**Daughter of the Prophet**

• •

Waajida	Finder
Waheede	Only one
Waseema	Pretty
Wattan	Homeland

• •

Yaasmeen	Jasmine
Yaella	Prominent
Yasmin	Jasmine
Yesenia	Flower
Yiesha	Woman of life

• •

Zaahida	Ascetic
Zaa'ira	Guest
Zaakira	Remembrance
Zada	Lucky
Zafina	Victorious

The 99 Glorious Names of Allah
··· *64* ···

Zahira	Luminous
Zahra	Blossom
Zahreh	Happiness
Zaida	Lucky
Zainab	Daughter of the Prophet
Zakia	Bright, pure
Zakkiyya	Intellectual
Zamurrad	Emerald
Zara	Princess
Zarifa	Graceful
Zarreen	Golden
Zayda	Fortunate
Zubaidah	High hill

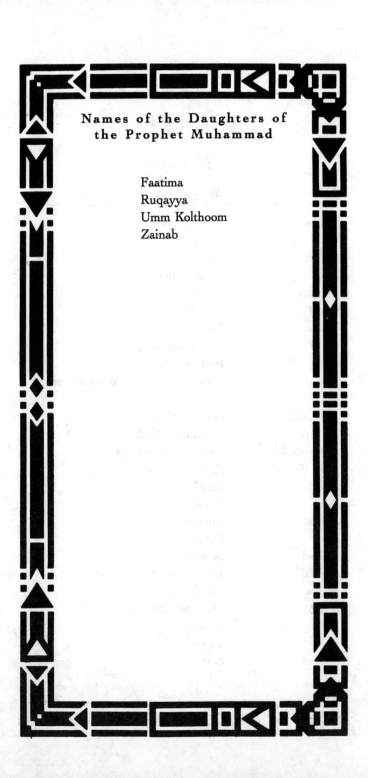

Names of the Daughters of the Prophet Muhammad

Faatima
Ruqayya
Umm Kolthoom
Zainab

$\mathscr{A}$RABIC

Male

Name	Meaning
'Aabid	Worshipper
'Aaftaab	Independent
'Aalim	Wise
Aamir	Commander
'Aaquil	Intelligent
'Aarif	Devotee
'Aashiq	Lover
'Aatif	Compassionate
Abdegalil	Slave of God
Abdul	Servant of (used with names of the Prophet)
Abdulaziz	Slave of God
Abdullah	Servant of Allah
Abdur-Rabb	Servant of the Lord
'Abu Kamal	Father of Kamal
Adeeb	Scholar
'Adil	Equal
Afdhal	Prominent
Afsar	Officer
Ahkeel	Intelligent
Ahmed	Praiseworthy
Ahsan	Handsome
Ajmal	More beautiful
Akbar	Greater
Akeel	Thoughtful
Akhtar	Star

Akil	Intelligent
Akmal	Complete
Akram	Merciful
'Ala	Glorious
Alasid	Lion
Aleem	Wise
Aleser	From As'ad
Alim	Learned
Altaaf	Grace and kindness
Altair	Flying eagle
Amal	Hope
Ameer	Ruler or prince
Amir	Prince
Amit	Most praised
Ammaad	Gift
Anas	Affection
Anees	Companion
Antuwain	Inestimable
Antwan	Variation of Antuwain
Anwaar	Multiple lights
Anwar	Luminous
Anwar	Beautiful
Aqeel	Intellectual
Arshad	Most honest
Asad	Lion
Asadel	Most prosperous one
'Asid	Variation of Asad
Ashfaaq	Compassion
Ashraf	Noble
'Askaree	Fighter
Aswad	Black
Athar	Pious
A'zam	Greatest
Azeem	Defender

Azhar	Evident
Azim	Defender
'Aziz	Variation of Azim
'Azmat	Greatness

. . . .

Baaqar	**Genius**
Badar	Full moon
Bahaadar	Brave
Bahaadur	Brave
Bahakaat	Prosperity
Bahraam	The planet Mars
Bakhtaawar	Fortunate
Ben-Ahmed	Son of Ahmed
Bilal	Chosen

. . . .

Cemal	**Beauty**
Charaagh	Light
Coman	Noble

. . . .

Daa'im	**Enduring**
Daanaa	Wise
Daanish	Knowing
Dalair	Valiant
Dawud	Form of David
Dekel	Date palm tree
Dhaigham	Lion
Dhameer	Heart
Dhiaa'	Splendid
Dilaawar	Daring

. . . .

E'jazz	Miracle
E'timaad	Trustworthy

. . . .

Faadhil	Abundant
Faa'ia	Excellent
Faakhir	Excellent
Faarih	Happy
Faarooq	Distinguished
Fadil	Generous
Faheem	Learned
Fairoze	Victorious
Faisal	Decisive
Falaah	Progress
Fareed	Unique
Faseeh	Eloquent
Fath	Victory
Fawaad	Heart

. . . .

Gadi	My fortune
Gadiel	Variation of Gadi
Ghaalib	Conqueror
Ghaazee	Hero
Ghassan	Family name of unknown meaning
Ghauth	Saint
Ghiyaath	Aid

. . . .

Haafiz	Governor
Haakim	Ruler
Haamid	One who praises

Haarith	Watchman
Haaziq	Skillful
Habib	Beloved
Hadad	Virility
Haidar	Lion
Hakim	Ruler
Halder	Lion
Halim	Gentle, mild
Hamal	Lamb
Hamdrem	Greatly praised
Hamdun	From Mohammed
Hamid	From Mohammed
Hammad	From Mohammed
Hamza	Lion
Hanee	Delighted
Haneef	True believer
Hanif	Variation of Haneef
Hannan	Compassionate
Harb	War
Harith	Ploughman
Harithah	From Harith
Harun	Teaching or singing
Hasan	Handsome
Hashim	Destroyer of evil
Hashmat	Dignified
Hassan	Handsome
Hidaayat	Guidance
Hilel	The new moon
Humayd	From Mohammed
Husain	Beautiful
Hussein	Little beauty

• •

Ibn-Mustapha	Son of Mustapha

Ibraar	Sainted
Ibrahim	From Abraham
Iftikhaar	Honored
Ihsaan	Benevolent
Ihtishaam	Magnificent
Ikhlaaq	Virtuous
Ikhlass	Sincere
Imaam	Leader
Iman	Faithful
Imran	Host
Iqbaal	Prosperous
Iqtidaar	Powerful
Iskandar	Defender of men
Islaam	Peaceful
Israar	Secrecy

· ·

Jaabir	Powerful
Jaalib	Importer
Ja'far	Rivulet
Jalaal	Grandeur
Jalees	Companion
Jamaal	Beauty, grace
Jamaine	A German
Jamal	Handsome
Jameel	Beautiful
Jamel	Variation of Jamal
Jaraad	Bountiful
Jauhar	Jewel

· ·

Kaashif	Discoverer
Kaatib	Writer
Kaazim	Restrainer

Kadar	Powerful
Kade	From Kadar
Kadin	Friend or confidante
Kadir	Green
Kafeel	Security
Kalb	From Caleb
Kaleem	Interlocutor
Kalil	Good friend
Kaliq	Creative
Kamaal	Perfection
Kamil	Variation of Kamaal
Karaamat	Miracle
Karam	Magnaminity
Kardal	Mustard seed
Kareem	Distinguished
Karraar	Impetuous
Kaseem	Variation of Kasim
Kasib	Fertile
Kasim	Divided
Katheer	Plentiful
Kaukab	Star
Kauthar	Abundant
Kedar	Powerful
Khaalid	Unforgettable
Khaalis	Pure
Khair	Charitable
Khalaf	Successor
Khaleefa	Caliph
Khaleell	Friend
Khaleeq	Competent
Khalil	Good friend
Khateeb	Orator
Khayyaam	Tentmaker
Khidar	Guide, leader

Khurran	Delightful
Khursheed	The sun
Kilab	From Caleb

• •

Laa'iq	Deserving
La'eeq	Able-bodied
Liaaqat	Fitness

• •

Ma'bood	Adored
Mahboob	Beloved friend
Mahomet	From Mohammed
Mahmud	Commendable
Majazz	Law-abiding
Maimun	Lucky
Malak	Divine messenger
Malik	Master
Mannaan	Generous
Mansur	Victorious
Manzoor	Admired
Maqbool	Chosen
Marghoob	Agreeable
Marid	Rebellious
Marjaan	Coral, seed pearls
Ma'roof	Celebrity
Marwan	Meaning unknown
Masaalih	Mediator
Ma'shooq	Sweetheart
Mas'ood	Lucky
Ma'soom	Innocent
Masroor	Happy
Matloob	Sought after
Maulaa	Master

Mazin	Surname used as a first name
Meer	Chief
Mehemet	Greatly praised
Miftaah	Keeper of the key
Misbaah	Light
Mohamet	From Mohammed
Mohammad	Variation of Mohammed
Mohammadi	From Mohammed
Mohammed	Name of the Prophet
Moonus	Consoler
Mu'azzam	Respected
Mubaarik	Blessed
Mu'eem	Helper
Muhaafiz	Protector
Mujahid	Warrior
Mukhtaar	Authorized
Munawwar	Illuminated
Mun'im	Generous
Munsif	Equitable
Muntasir	Triumphant
Muqaddas	Sanctified
Mureed	Disciple
Mursal	Envoy
Murshid	Leader
Musharraf	Honored
Mustafah	Chosen one
Mutaqaddim	Predecessor
Muttagee	Pious
Muzaffar	Victorious

· ·

Naadir	Rare
Naa'ib	Delegate
Naaji'	Useful

Naasi'	Clear
Naasih	Advisor
Naazi'	Foreigner
Naazim	Administrator
Naazir	Observant
Nabeel	Magnanimous
Nabil	Variation of Nabeel
Nadeem	Courtier
Na'eem	Happiness
Nafees	Exquisite
Najam	Fortunate
Najee'	Beneficial
Najeeb	Excellent
Najib	Of noble descent
Naqee	Pure
Naqeeb	Proclaimer
Naqqaash	Artist
Naseer	Assistant
Nasser	Victorious
Nawwaab	Ruler
Nayyir	Shining
Nazar	Gift
Ni'mat	Blessing
Nishaat	Energetic
Numa	Pleasant
Numair	Panther
Nusair	Vulture

· ·

Peer	Leader
Pervaiz	King of Persia

Names of the Prophet

Name	Meaning
'Aadil	Just
Aamir	Commander
'Aaqib	Terminator
'Abdullah	Man of Allah
Ahmad	Commendable
Ameen	Honest
Basheer	Precurser
Daa'	Motive
Faatih	Conquerer
Haad	Leader
Haamid	Thankful
Habeeb-ullah	Sweetheart of Allah
Jawwaad	Generous
Khaatim	Seal
Khaleel	Intimate
Maah	Threadbare
Ma'aloom	Famous
Maamoon	Trustworthy
Mad'oo	Pretender
Mahdee	Leader
Mahmood	Praiseworthy
Mansoor	Victorious
Mashhood	Proved
Mateen	Solid
Mubashshir	Evangelist
Mubeen	Evident

Muhammad	Praiseworthy
Muharram	Sacred
Mujtabaa	Selected
Mukarram	Honored
Munajj	Saviour
Muneer	Luminous
Muqtasid	Wise
Murtadhaa	Chosen
Musaddiq	Credible
Mustafaa	Chosen
Mutahhar	Purifier
Mutee'	Willing
Muzakkir	Reminder
Naah	Prohibitor
Nabee	Prophet
Najee-ullah	Confidante of Allah
Nazeer	Forerunner
Qaasim	Distributor
Qareeb	Close
Rasool	Messenger
Saadiq	Truthful
Sayyed	Chief
Shaaf	Healer
Shaahid	Witness
Shaheed	Martyr
Shaheer	Famous
Siraaj	Night Lamp
Tayyab	Chaste

· ·

Qaahir	Victorious
Qaa'im	Erect
Qaani'	Content
Qaaree	Reader

Qabil	Able
Qadeer	Powerful
Qadim	Ancient
Qadir	Powerful
Qaiser	Emperor
Qamar	The moon
Qudrat	Powerful
Qutab	Pivot

· ·

Raaghib	**Willing**
Raahat	Restful
Raaqim	Writer
Raashid	Conscious
Raasikh	Stable
Raaziq	Provider
Rabb	Master
Ra'ees	Head or chief
Rafee'	Exalted
Rafeeq	Kind
Rafi	From Raphael
Rahman	Merciful
Rahmat	Mercy
Rasool	Messenger
Raushan	Bright as a star
Rayhan	Favored by God

· ·

Sa'aadat	**Felicity**
Saabir	Patient
Sa'ad	Fortunate
Saagh	Jeweler
Saahib	Friend
Saajid	Worshipper

Saalih	Virtuous
Saalim	Safe
Saami'	Listener
Sabeeh	Radiant
Sabooh	Cheerful
Saddam	Meaning unknown
Sadiq	Truthful
Sa'eed	Lucky
Safee	Honest
Safeer	Ambassador
Sa'id	Happy
Saif	Sword
Sajjad	Worshipper of Allah
Sakhaawat	Generous
Salaah	Goodness
Salaamat	Peaceful
Salih	Right or good
Salik	Follower of spiritual path
Salim	Secure
Samein	God heard
Samir	Entertainer
Samman	Grocer
Sammon	Variation of Samman
Sardaar	Commander
Sarraaf	Treasurer
Sarwar	Chief
Seif	Sword of religion
Sibt	Grandson
Siddeeq	Righteous
Sidq	Truth
Seemaab	Mercury
Shaab	Happy
Shaafi'	Preemptor
Shaah	King

Shaaheen	Hawk or falcon
Shaakir	Content
Shaari'	Legislator
Shaatir	Clever
Shafee'	Patron
Shafeeq	Compassionate
Shaikh	Chef
Shakeei	Handsome
Sharaafat	Well mannered
Shareef	Noble
Sharif	Variation of Shareef
Shujaa'	Courageous
Siddeeq	Righteous
Siraj	Night lamp
Sofian	Devoted
Sultaan	Monarch
Syed	Happy

· ·

Taahir	**Pure**
Taajwar	Prince
Taalib	Seeker
Taariq	Morning star
Tahir	Variation of Taahir
Tajammal	Beauty
Talib	Student
Tanweer	Enlightened
Taqqee	Pious
Tasaddaq	Almsgiving
Tasawwar	Imaginative
Taufeeq	Prosperous
Tauqeer	Honorable
Tayib	Good or delicate
Thaaqib	Glistening

Thamar	Profitable
Timin	Sea serpent
Tufail	Mediator

. . . .

'Umar	Life
Usama	Lion

. . . .

Waahib	Liberal
Waaiz	Preacher
Waathiq	Confident
Waheed	Unique
Wahhaj	Glowing
Wajaahat	High position
Waseem	Handsome
Wazeer	Minister
Wazir	Variation of Wazeer
Wiqaar	Dignified

. . . .

Yaameen	Towards right
Yaawar	Aide-de-camp
Yahya	Living
Yardan	King
Yasar	Wealth
Yaseen	Name of a chapter in the Koran
Yasir	Variation of Yasar
Yazid	His power and influence will grow
Yusef	Form of Joseph

. . . .

Zahid	Ascetic
Zaim	Brigadier general

Zaki	Bright or pure
Zayn	Ornamental
Zimraan	Celebrated

Biblical Names and Arabic Equivalents

Arabs and Christians have a shared history and there are often equivalents of biblical names. Here are a few.

Name	Equivalent
Aaron	Haaroon
Abel	Haabeel
Abraham	Ibraaheem
Adam	Aadam
Cain	Qaabeel
David	Daa'ood
Enoch	Idrees
Gabriel	Jibreel
Isaac	Ishaaq
Jacob	Ya'qoob
Jesus	'Eesaa
Job	Ayyoob
John	Yahyaa
Joseph	Yoosuf
Moses	Moosaa
Noah	Nooh
Solomon	Sulaimaan

CHINESE NAMES

The choosing of names in the Chinese-speaking world is of the utmost importance. The Chinese have made an art—even a science—of this cultural imperative, believing that a person's name will have far-reaching effects upon his life and influence him mentally through invisible psychological means. If, for example, a child is called Fatty all the days of his youth, he will suffer low self-esteem and attendant problems. On the other hand, if he is called Handsome, he is likely to develop a very high opinion of himself.

It is the belief that a child's innate intelligence and spirit will be fused with the name he is given as he will hear, think, and write his name all the days of his life. Thus, his character and emotions will be unconsciously influenced by the meaning inherent in his name. His fate, too, can be influenced this way.

A person's name also serves as an image-maker in the minds of others, especially in today's image-conscious, media-driven world. The Chinese have known for centuries that people's names usher in the first impression about them.

There is a Chinese saying, "A tiger leaves its skin after death, so does a person his name." Thus the sight or sound of a person's name recalls his life and deeds. The name Thomas Jefferson brings to mind an entire period of history; the name Judas bespeaks treachery. It is most important to the Chinese to choose a name that has good connotations and to avoid those with negative implications. Another Chinese proverb goes, "One is not afraid to be born with a bad destiny but to be given a bad name."

Everywhere in the Orient, Chinese characters are mutually intelligible to literate people no matter what their language or dialect. For this reason, Chinese literature that is thousands of years old can be read today by anyone fluent in Chinese. Thus the characters are an integral part of the naming process. These are chosen, after careful thought and consideration, not only for the meaning of the name and its sound, but also for the art and beauty of the calligraphy. Through the shapes of the characters, Chinese names convey design and beauty visually as well as harmonious sound and uplifting meaning.

The versatility of different combinations can be used to express subtle shades of meaning and these meanings can indicate the parents' aspirations for this child as well as their philosophical outlook on life. It is therefore important for names to be easy to write and to remember.

Most Chinese given names are of two characters. The listing which follows provides a sampling of some of the thousands of Chinese words used for names. To create a name, pick two different names and combine them. For example, Ah Die, like a butterfly, is made up of Ah, like a and Die, "butterfly." Ah Tao would be like a peach.

Since Chinese parents create an original name for each child, few names are identical and there is no such thing as a common name, such as John or

Mary. In addition, family names are likely to bear a resemblance. For example, two sisters might be named Mu Lan (magnolia blossom) and Mu Tan (tree peony blossom). Another family might choose Li Hua (pear blossom) and Kuai (mallow blossom) for its daughters.

The true Chinese name is a unique creation meant to embody the parents' ideals and hopes and the traditional values of the culture—loyalty, respect for one's elders, trustworthiness, peaceableness, exemplary behavior, and the bringing of honor to one's ancestors.

The surname, too, is part of this interwoven process. The given name must complement the surname, which is written first. Most surnames are limited to one character. An example of a well-chosen complete name might be Cheng Zhongshi: Cheng means success; Zhong, the end; and Shi, the beginning. Thus, success from beginning to end. A bright wish to carry through life!

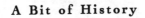

A Bit of History

The presence of Chinese people in the New World occurred as early as the middle of the 16th century when they were employed as servants to the invading Spanish fleet. By 1635 there were some Chinese colonists in Mexico, but the major influx did not arrive until the second half of the 19th century when severe drought in the Canton province drove thousands to seek their fortunes in America. Between 1847 and 1850, Chinese immigrants followed the gold rush miners, often making their living doing laundry, which was considered "woman's work," and disdained by the rough miners. In offering this essential, but looked-down-upon service, the Chinese became their own bosses.

From 1858–1869 thousands of Chinese helped build the California railroads, the western link of the transcontinental rail system that tied America together from sea to shining sea. Doing dangerous and dirty work under hazardous conditions, the Chinese often made up as much as 90 percent of the workforce although they were paid much less than the white laborers.

As California's agriculture grew, and cheap labor was needed, the number of Chinese immigrants grew, ensured by a treaty with China in 1868 which permitted the immigration of Chinese laborers. During this period, approximately 12,000 Chinese immigrated each year, mostly to California, where they were also hired in silver and coal mines, canneries, cigar and shoe factories, woolen mills, and the garment industry.

By 1870, the Caucasian population clamored to take back jobs held by the Chinese. Their efforts resulted in the Chinese Exclusion Act of 1882, prohibiting immigration for ten years. This law was extended twice, resulting in a policy of almost total exclusion of Chinese workers. The act remained in force until 1943 when the manpower shortages of World War II again made imported labor necessary.

Although 19th-century immigrants were almost exclusively men, Chinese women began to immigrate in large numbers as wives and fiancees of GIs, returning from the war and as mail-order brides for Chinese men.

In 1965 immigration restrictions were lifted and families, long separated, began to reunite in the United States. The immigration numbers rose dramatically. During the 1950s fewer than 1,000 Chinese had come annually; by the 1980s as many as 30,000 per year arrived.

Today there are thriving and growing communities of Chinese in many places. Although the famous Chinatowns of San

Francisco and New York remain the hub of Chinese life in America and the first port of call, Chinese have migrated across the land bringing their unique culture with them.

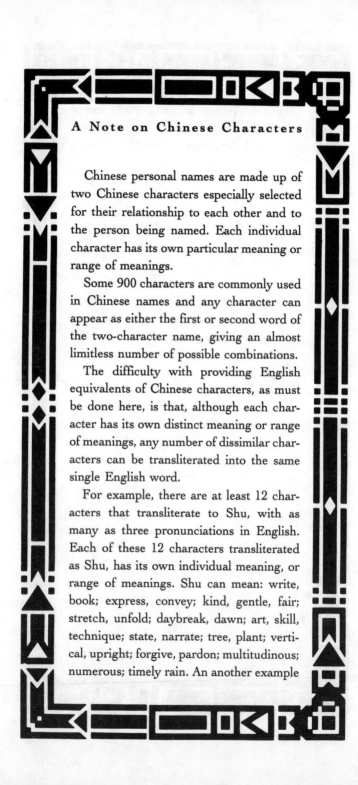

A Note on Chinese Characters

Chinese personal names are made up of two Chinese characters especially selected for their relationship to each other and to the person being named. Each individual character has its own particular meaning or range of meanings.

Some 900 characters are commonly used in Chinese names and any character can appear as either the first or second word of the two-character name, giving an almost limitless number of possible combinations.

The difficulty with providing English equivalents of Chinese characters, as must be done here, is that, although each character has its own distinct meaning or range of meanings, any number of dissimilar characters can be transliterated into the same single English word.

For example, there are at least 12 characters that transliterate to Shu, with as many as three pronunciations in English. Each of these 12 characters transliterated as Shu, has its own individual meaning, or range of meanings. Shu can mean: write, book; express, convey; kind, gentle, fair; stretch, unfold; daybreak, dawn; art, skill, technique; state, narrate; tree, plant; vertical, upright; forgive, pardon; multitudinous; numerous; timely rain. An another example

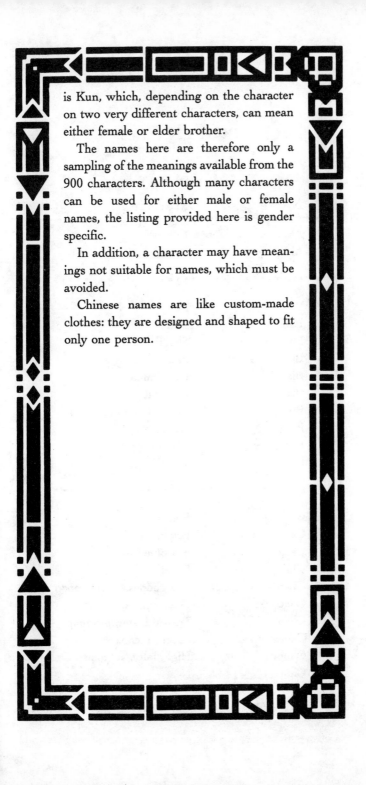

is Kun, which, depending on the character on two very different characters, can mean either female or elder brother.

The names here are therefore only a sampling of the meanings available from the 900 characters. Although many characters can be used for either male or female names, the listing provided here is gender specific.

In addition, a character may have meanings not suitable for names, which must be avoided.

Chinese names are like custom-made clothes: they are designed and shaped to fit only one person.

CHINESE

Female

Name	Meaning
Ah	Like a
Ai	Friendly

. . . .

Name	Meaning
Bai	Pure
Bao	Bud
Bei	Shellfish
Bi	Jade
Bian	Discriminate
Biao	Example
Bin	Refined and courteous
Bing	Ice
Bo	Wave
Bu	Walk

. . . .

Name	Meaning
Cai	Splendid
Can	Bright
Cang	Sea blue
Chan	Lovely
Chang	The goddess of the moon
Chao	Tide
Chen	Treasure, star, morning
Cheng	Succeed, capable
Chong	High, lofty, sublime
Chu	Neat

Chuan	River
Chun	Spring, pure
Chuo	Ample
Ci	Tenderhearted
Cong	Bright, intelligent
Cui	Resplendent

. . . .

Da	Eldest
Dai	A black pigment
Dan	Dawn
Dao	Lead, guide
De	Heart, mind
Deng	Light
Di	Bamboo flute
Dian	Standard, ceremony
Die	Butterfly
Ding	Calm, stable
Dong	Direct
Du	Sincere
Duan	Upright, proper
Duo	Much, more, many

. . . .

E	Pretty young woman
En	Favor, grace
Er	Jade or pearl earring

. . . .

Fan	Buddhist
Fang	Fragrant
Fei	Luxuriant
Fen	Sweet smell, fragrant
Feng	Elegant

Fo	Buddhist
Fu	Lotus

. . . .

Gan	**S**weet
Gao	Tall
Ge	Pattern, style
Gen	Root, base
Geng	Honest
Gong	Respectful
Gu	Valley
Guan	The best
Guang	Light, brightness
Gui	Precious
Guo	Fruit, result

. . . .

Hai	**S**ea
Han	Calligraphy
Hao	Luminous
He	Harmony
Heng	Constant
Hong	Rainbow
Hu	Lake
Hua	Blossom
Huai	Bosom
Huan	Joyous
Huang	Phoenix
Hui	Orchid

. . . .

Ji	Lucky
Jia	Beautiful
Jian	Strong

Jiao	Charming
Jie	With all one's heart
Jin	Gold
Jing	Crystal
Jiong	Shining
Jlu	For a long time
Ju	Chrysanthemum
Juan	Graceful
Jue	Two pieces of Jade

• •

Kai	Open, start
Kang	Fervent, generous
Ke	A jadelike stone
Ken	Earnestly, sincerely
Kong	Sky, air
Kuan	Happy
Kui	Sunflower
Kun	Female

• •

Lai	Come, arrive
Lan	Orchid
Lang	Light, bright
Le	Cheerful
Lei	Flower bud
Li	Pear
Lian	Lotus
Liang	Enlightened
Liao	Faraway, vast
Lin	Beautiful jade
Ling	Dainty
Liu	Willow
Lu	Dew

Luan	A small tinkling bell
Luo	Name of a river

• •

Ma	**A**gate
Mai	Wheat
Man	Trailing plant
Mang	Rays of light
Mao	Luxuriant
Mei	Rose, plum blossom
Meng	Dream
Mi	Honey, sweet
Mian	Continuous, unbroken
Miao	Wonderful
Min	Keen
Ming	Brilliant
Mo	Jasmine
Mu	Harmonious

• •

Na	**E**njoy
Nai	To bear or endure
Nan	South
Neng	Ability
Ni	Girl
Nian	A period of life
Ning	Tranquil
Nuan	Genial

• •

Pa	**F**lower
Pei	Abundant
Peng	Friend
Pi	Stringed musical instrument

Pian	Trippingly
Ping	Apple
Pu	Uncut jade

. . . .

Qi	Fine jade
Qian	Courteous
Qiao	Ingenious
Qin	Celery
Qing	Blue or green
Qiong	Fine jade
Qiu	Autumn
Qu	Delight
Quan	Perfect
Que	True, reliable
Qun	The masses

. . . .

Ran	Right, correct
Ren	Kindhearted
Rong	Cotton rose
Rou	Soft, tender
Ru	Like, as, if
Rui	Wise
Run	Moist, smooth, sleek
Ruo	Like, seem, if

. . . .

Sai	Surpass
Se	A musical instrument
Sen	Forest
Sha	A type of grass
Shan	Coral
Shang	Esteem

Shao	Beautiful springtime
Shen	Cautious
Sheng	Holy, a sage
Shi	Poetry
Shou	Teacher
Shu	Gentle, fair
Shui	Water, river
Shun	Smooth, unhindered
Shuo	Twinkle
Shuo	New moon
Si	Silk
Song	Praise, song
Su	Simple
Sui	Peaceful

. . . .

Tai	Peaceful
Tan	Pond
Tang	Stately, dignified
Tao	Peach
Te	Special
Ti	Body
Tian	Sweet, honeyed
Ting	Graceful
Tong	Phoenix tree
Tu	Picture
Tuan	Round, circular
Tuo	Proper, appropriate

. . . .

Wan	Gentle, gracious
Wang	Flourishing
Wei	Rare treasure
Wen	Gentle, cultivated

Wo	Fertile
Wu	Chinese parasol

. . . .

Xi	**R**are, uncommon
Xia	Rosy clouds
Xian	Refined, elegant
Xiang	Sunny
Xiao	Dawn
Xie	Harmonious
Xin	Star
Xing	Apricot or almond
Xiu	First-rate
Xu	Brilliance of the rising sun
Xuan	Mysterious
Xue	Snow
Xun	Swift

. . . .

Ya	**P**roper, correct
Yan	Bright red
Yang	Ocean
Yao	Gentle and graceful
Ye	Leaf
Yi	Cheerful
Yin	Silver
Ying	Cherry
Yong	Elegant and poised
You	Excellence
Yu	Feather
Yuan	Erudite
Yue	The moon
Yun	Cloud

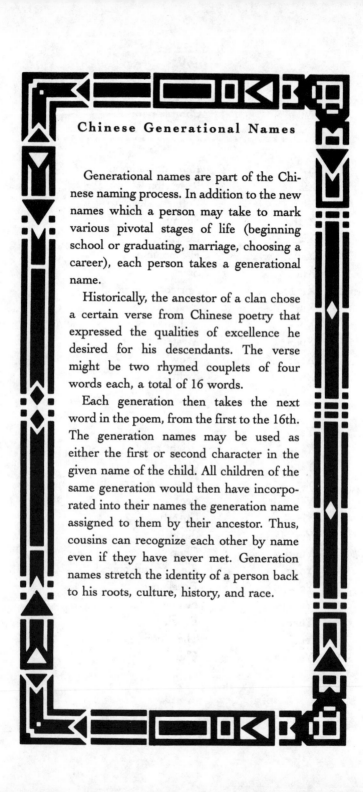

Chinese Generational Names

Generational names are part of the Chinese naming process. In addition to the new names which a person may take to mark various pivotal stages of life (beginning school or graduating, marriage, choosing a career), each person takes a generational name.

Historically, the ancestor of a clan chose a certain verse from Chinese poetry that expressed the qualities of excellence he desired for his descendants. The verse might be two rhymed couplets of four words each, a total of 16 words.

Each generation then takes the next word in the poem, from the first to the 16th. The generation names may be used as either the first or second character in the given name of the child. All children of the same generation would then have incorporated into their names the generation name assigned to them by their ancestor. Thus, cousins can recognize each other by name even if they have never met. Generation names stretch the identity of a person back to his roots, culture, history, and race.

. . . .

Zai	To be living
Zan	Praise, agree
Ze	Moist, glossy
Zeng	Increase, gain
Zhan	Spread the wings
Zhao	Spirit, vigor
Zhen	Treasure, precious
Zheng	Honest
Zhi	Irises and orchids
Zhong	Second in order of birth
Zhu	Pearl, jewel
Zhuan	Expert
Zhuang	Serious, grave
Zhuo	Luminous
Zi	Purple, violet
Zong	Palm
Zu	Earliest ancestor
Zuo	Polish, refine

Chinese Equivalents of English Names

English names vary from one to four syllables, while Chinese names are almost invariably only two characters. Therefore, Chinese equivalents are always two characters. Here are a few examples:

Name	Equivalent
Alexander	Li Da, An De, Shang Da
Amanda	Ming Da, Meng De, Meng Da
Bobby	Bo Fu, Bo Bi, Bo Bei
Caroline	Kan Rong, Ruo Lin, Kai Ling
Janet	Zhen Yi, Jing Yi, Jian Ni
Lisa	Li Sha, Li Shan, Li Sa
Natalie	Le Di, Na Li, Nai Qian
Teddy	Tai De, Tai Di, De Di

$\mathscr{C}$HINESE

Male

Name	Meaning
An	Peaceful, calm
Ang	High-spirited

. . . .

Bai	Cypress
Ban	Class, team
Bang	Nation, state
Bao	Praise, honor
Bei	North
Ben	The root of a plant
Bi	Green jade
Bian	Discriminating
Biao	Young tiger
Bin	Refined and courteous
Bing	Soldier
Bo	Eldest brother
Bu	Walk, go on foot

. . . .

Cai	Talented
Can	Splendid
Cang	Dark green pines
Cao	Conduct
Ce	Plan, scheme
Chang	Prosperous
Chao	Tide

Chen	Treasure
Cheng	Sincere, honest
Chi	Discreet
Chong	Substantial
Chu	The stone base of a column
Chuan	River
Chuang	Achieve
Chun	Pure
Cong	Intelligent
Cui	Resplendent

. . . .

Da	**D**istinguished
Dai	Hawksbill turtle
Dan	Red
Dao	Lead, guide
De	Virtue
Deng	Ascend
Di	Enlighten
Dian	Model, type
Ding	Able-bodied man
Dong	Master
Du	Sincere
Duan	Upright
Dun	Honest
Duo	Much, more, many

. . . .

En	**K**indness, favor, grace
Er	Son

. . . .

Fa	**D**evelop, grow, sprout
Fan	Sail

Fang	Upright
Fei	Striking
Fen	Exert oneself, raise, lift
Feng	Handsome
Fo	Buddha
Fu	Husband

· ·

Gan	**B**old, daring
Gang	Firm, strong
Gao	Tall, high
Ge	Standard, pattern
Gen	Root, base
Geng	Honest and just
Gong	Capable
Gu	Resolute
Guan	Champion
Guang	Honor, glory
Gui	Noble
Guo	Resolute

· ·

Hai	**S**ea
Han	Self-restraint
Hao	Heroic spirit
He	River
Heng	Prosperity
Hong	Magnificent
Hou	Nobleman
Hu	Tiger
Hua	Best part (the cream)
Huai	Chinese scholar
Huan	Joyous
Huang	Phoenix

| Hui | Splendor |

. . . .

Ji	**A**ccomplishment
Jia	Increase
Jian	Firm, solid
Jiao	Teach, instruct
Jie	Prominent
Jin	Vigorous
Jing	Tranquility
Jiong	Bright, shining
Jlu	For a long time
Ju	Raise, hold up
Juan	Meaningful
Jun	Hero

. . . .

Kai	**T**riumphant
Kang	Well-being
Ke	Able
Ken	Consent
Kong	Sky, air
Kuan	Well-off
Kui	Stalwart
Kun	Elder brother

. . . .

Lai	Future
Lan	Haze, mist
Lang	Light, bright
Lao	Service
Le	Joyful
Lei	Thunder
Li	Upright

Lian	Ally oneself with
Liang	Able person
Liao	Faraway, vast
Lie	Strong, raging fire
Lin	Good soaking rain
Ling	Quick, clever
Liu	Willow
Long	Grand, thriving
Lu	Land
Luan	Mountain
Lun	Logic, order
Luo	Name of a river

· ·

Ma	Agate
Mai	Advance with big strides
Man	Well-filled
Mang	Brilliant light
Mao	Diligent
Meng	Eldest brother
Mi	Overflowing
Mian	Continuous
Miao	Young plant, seedling
Min	Famous
Ming	Bright, brilliant
Mo	Standard, model
Mu	Tree, wood

· ·

Na	Receive
Nai	Endurance
Nan	Man
Neng	Capability
Nian	Year, age

Ning	Peaceful
Nong	Farming

· ·

Pan	**Huge rock**
Pang	Large
Pei	Abundant
Peng	A bright future
Pin	Moral character
Ping	Calm, quiet
Pu	Uncut jade

· ·

Qi	**Wonderful**
Qian	Thousand
Qiang	Powerful
Qiao	Tall
Qin	Industrious
Qing	Stainless
Qiong	Fine jade
Qu	Interest, delight
Quan	Power, authority
Que	Reliable
Qun	The masses

· ·

Ran	**Correct**
Ren	Benevolent
Rong	Harmonious
Ru	Like, as if
Rui	Auspicious
Run	Sleek
Ruo	Like, seem

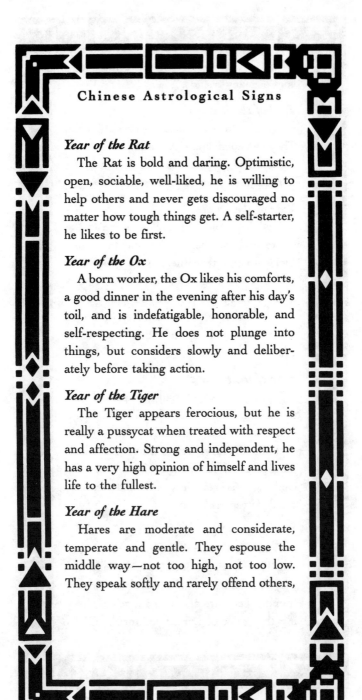

Chinese Astrological Signs

Year of the Rat

The Rat is bold and daring. Optimistic, open, sociable, well-liked, he is willing to help others and never gets discouraged no matter how tough things get. A self-starter, he likes to be first.

Year of the Ox

A born worker, the Ox likes his comforts, a good dinner in the evening after his day's toil, and is indefatigable, honorable, and self-respecting. He does not plunge into things, but considers slowly and deliberately before taking action.

Year of the Tiger

The Tiger appears ferocious, but he is really a pussycat when treated with respect and affection. Strong and independent, he has a very high opinion of himself and lives life to the fullest.

Year of the Hare

Hares are moderate and considerate, temperate and gentle. They espouse the middle way—not too high, not too low. They speak softly and rarely offend others,

which makes them likeable and the posses-
sors of many friends.

Year of the Dragon

Dragons are the luckiest of all people.
They can command riches and power, good
fortune and long life. Visionaries, they can
nonetheless pursue a goal relentlessly.

Year of the Snake

Snake people are lucky because the
snake is a member of the dragon family.
Once upon a time there were temples in
China to the dragon and the snake, who is
a universal symbol for wisdom and perspi-
cacity. Snake people are talented and have
an indominitable spirit which leads them
eventually to success.

Year of the Horse

Horse people are broad-minded and easy
to get along with. They like to be on the go
and seem to be constantly in movement.
Optimistic and cheerful, they may lack
perseverance. Known as bigmouths, they
can't keep secrets very well and tend towards irresponsibility.

Year of the Goat

Goats are generally good-natured and
they like marriage. Sociable and peaceable,
they are fond of social life and have many
friends. They are also humanitarians, having the "milk of human kindness." Often

they are of a strikingly elegant appearance
and exhibit grace.

Year of the Monkey

Monkeys are considered to be fickle-
minded and easily irritated—in other words
they get bored quickly. Bright and cunning,
they respond to flattery and will go to great
lengths to get attention. Quick-witted and
able, they are not above dishonesty.

Year of the Cock

Cocks are, as the name implies, full of
self-confidence and pride. They work hard
and systematically, bringing both attention
to detail and enthusiasm to their work.
Tactful and fond of self-adornment, cocks
are good negotiators.

Year of the Dog

Dog people usually do fairly well in life.
They are loyal and clever, intuitive and
faithful. They must work hard for their
living but they often perform extraordinary
works. The dog can be psychic, as he
follows an invisible trail with his nose, and
he likes people.

Year of the Pig

Pigs like to spend money and they tend
to eat too much. Although they can be
selfish, they have leadership qualities and
high standards. They like their physical
comforts and have a tendency to sloth.

Birth Years and Corresponding Astrological Signs

Rat	1900	1912	1924	1936	1948	1960	1972	1984
Ox	1901	1913	1925	1937	1949	1961	1973	1985
Tiger	1902	1914	1926	1938	1950	1962	1974	1986
Hare	1903	1915	1927	1939	1951	1963	1975	1987
Dragon	1904	1916	1928	1940	1952	1964	1976	1988
Snake	1905	1917	1929	1941	1953	1965	1977	1989
Horse	1906	1918	1930	1942	1954	1966	1978	1990
Goat	1907	1919	1931	1943	1955	1967	1979	1991
Monkey	1908	1920	1932	1944	1956	1968	1980	1992
Cock	1909	1921	1933	1945	1957	1969	1981	1993
Dog	1910	1922	1934	1946	1958	1970	1982	1994
Pig	1911	1923	1935	1947	1959	1971	1983	1995

· ·

Sai	**Surpass**
Sen	Multitudinous
Shan	China fir
Shang	Forge ahead
Shao	Glorious youth
Shen	Gentleman
Sheng	Sage
Shi	Fruit, seed
Shou	Leader
Shu	Express, convey
Shui	River
Shun	Unhindered
Shuo	Great achievements
Si	Think, consider
Song	Lofty
Su	Respectful
Sui	Peaceful

· ·

Tai	**Highest**
Tan	Candid
Tang	Dignified
Tao	Crashing waves
Te	Special
Teng	Gallop, prance
Ti	Body
Tian	Heaven
Tie	Man of iron will
Ting	Palace, pavilion
Tong	Unobstructed, clear
Tu	Plan, pursue
Tuan	Reunion

Tuo	Appropriate

· ·

Wan	Ten thousand
Wang	King
Wei	Impressive strength
Wen	Gentle and cultivated
Wo	Fertile
Wu	Awaken

· ·

Xi	Uncommon
Xia	Just
Xian	Illustrious
Xiang	Auspicious
Xiao	Valiant
Xie	Harmonious
Xin	Flourishing
Xing	Rise, spring up
Xiong	Mighty, hero
Xiu	Mastery
Xu	Open-minded
Xuan	Imposing
Xue	Scholar
Xun	Achievement

· ·

Ya	Refined, correct
Yan	Handsome
Yang	The sun
Yao	Shine, dazzle
Ye	Professional work
Yi	Suitable, fitting
Yin	Wise, brilliant

Ying	Hawk, eagle
Yong	Valiant, courageous
You	First-rate
Yu	Happy, joyful
Yuan	Erudite
Yue	High mountain
Yun	Fair, just

. . . .

Zan	Support, praise
Ze	Duty
Zeng	Increase
Zhan	Far-seeing
Zhang	Jade tablet
Zhao	Vigorous
Zhe	Philosopher
Zhen	Genuine
Zheng	Honest and aboveboard
Zhi	Sincere, earnest
Zhong	Second born
Zhou	Boat
Zhu	Bamboo
Zhuan	Expert
Zhuang	Robust
Zhuo	Outstanding
Zi	Industrious
Zong	Palm
Zuo	Assist

JAPANESE NAMES

Japanese names are Chinese characters interpreted in a Japanese way. There are literally *thousands* of Japanese names, not all of which are easily translatable into English, and they come from a variety of sources including the combination of root words with prefixes and suffixes.

Many names are used for both boys and girls. Names of literary and historical figures are considered of great importance. And, in a land where Buddhism has held great sway, virtues implied in the Buddhist philosophy are deemed extremely desirable.

Thus, imbedded in many names with other ostensible meanings (such as Umeko meaning plum blossom, but implying wifely devotion) are implications of these Buddhistic virtues. Lotus, lotus blossom or water lily are not flowers merely but invoke the entire Buddhist concept of a lotus heaven where the departed souls sleep enfolded within lotus buds until they enter Buddha heaven.

Other nature or plant names have similar connotations. For example, cherry blossom (Sakura) implies wealth; slender bamboo (Shino), fidelity; and cedar (Sugi), moral rectitude.

Japanese girls' names often refer to typical Japanese virtues: Haruko meaning tranquil; Iku, nourishing; Ko, filial piety; Michiko, beauty and wisdom; and Ran, *purity*.

Other girls' names reflect the natural beauties that the Japanese prize and which play a large role in their culture. Chrysanthemum (Kiku), for example, is a favorite subject for artists as is the iris, or flower of the moon (Ayame). Probably the most famous of these nature names to English-speaking ears is that of Cho-cho san, or Madame Butterfly, from cho meaning butterfly.

Girls' names can be created by adding the suffixes, -ko, -yo, or -e to the listed name elements. Thus Kiku can become Kikuko or Ran could become Ranyo.

Number names are popular, too, though mostly for boys. Large round numbers (ten thousand or Man) are considered good omens. Chizu, meaning a thousand storks, is a name denoting longevity. Smaller numbers are used for birth order.

To create an original boy's name, you can use a prefix such as Masa (good), Zen (just), Toku (virtue), or Shin, (faithful). Masojiro, for example, means good second son, from Jiro which means second son. Similarly, Shinshiro combines Shin with Shiro (fourth-born son) to create faithful fourth-born son.

In addition, the suffix -o appears in male names, such as Toshio, year boy, Yukio, he goes his own way; or Seiko (variation of Sei), truth.

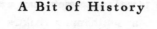

A Bit of History

Although Japan was first visited by Europeans (Portuguese) in 1542, by the early 1600s successors of the conquering shoguns cut off nearly all Japanese contact with foreigners; isolating the islands for hundreds of years.

The few Japanese who arrived on American shores before 1885 came accidentally as the result of being shipwrecked. But in 1885 the Japanese government began to allow its citizens to immigrate. The Chinese Exclusion Act of 1882 had prohibited Chinese from immigrating but it left the door open to Japanese laborers. Taking advantage of America's need for workers on the West Coast, the Japanese were willing to work for low wages, demand for them increased.

Then, in 1896, the Japanese government revised its immigration law. The new law required an emigrant to have someone responsible for his support should he become ill or unable to work. Because they themselves made little money, few Japanese families could vouch for the support of an emigrant, but a system soon arose where American companies interested in imported cheap labor provided the necessary financial guarantees, joining with agents in Japan, which secured the emigrants.

This system worked so successfully that

during a five-year period (1899–1904) some 60,000 Japanese came to America, settling primarily in Hawaii and on the West Coast. By 1920 approximately 220,000 Japanese resided in Hawaii and California. A total immigration population of 300,000 was recorded by 1924, though many of these eventually returned to Japan.

About this time, Caucasian residents on the West Coast began to fear that abundant Japanese labor would deprive them of their jobs. To avoid the panic that resulted in the Chinese Exclusion Act, the United States came to a "gentlemen's agreement" with Japan under which the Japanese government restricted the emigration of laborers.

Professionals and mail-order brides (also known as "picture brides," because of their prospective husbands chose them from photographs) were not included in the voluntary restrictions. This latter helped relieve the female to male imbalance of Japanese in America.

Despite these exceptions, the 1924 Immigration Act, which excluded immigrants who could never become citizens (at that time only whites and blacks were eligible for citizenship), reduced Japanese immigration to a virtual standstill until the end of World War II when Japanese brides of American soldiers began arriving in large numbers—a quarter of a million by 1960. Since then, the annual immigration volume from Japan has remained fairly steady at about 5,000 per year.

JAPANESE

Female

Name	Meaning
Ai	Love, indigo blue
Aiko	Little love, beloved
Akako	Red, a charm to cure disease
Akasuki	Bright, helper
Aki	Autumn born
Akina	Spring flower with bright leaves
Anzu	Apricot, feminine love
Aoi	Hollyhock
Asa	Morning born
Au	Meeting
Ayako	Damask pattern
Ayame	Iris, flower of the moon
Azami	Thistle (defiant)

. . . .

Chika	Near, in the sense of closeness
Chikako	Clever, wise
Chitose	Thousand years
Chizue	A thousand storks, longevity
Chizuko	Dimunitive of Chizue
Cho	Butterfly

. . . .

Dai	Great
Den	Bequest from ancestors

....

Etsu	Delight

....

Fuyu	Born in winter

....

Gen	Spring or source
Gin	Silver
Gina	Silvery

....

Hama	Shore
Hamako	Variation of Hama
Hana	Flower or blossom
Hanae	Blossom
Hanako	Fair
Haru	Spring born
Harue	Springtime bay
Haruko	Tranquil
Hatsu	First born
Haya	Quick, light
Hide	Excellent
Hideyo	Superior generations
Hiro	Broad
Hiroko	Magnanimous
Hisa	Long-lasting (longevity)
Hisae	Dimunitive of Hisa
Hisako	Variation of Hisa
Hisano	Long plain
Hisayo	Variation of Hisa
Hoshi	Star, a traditional name
Hoshie	Dimunitive of Hoshi

Hoshiko	Variation of Hoshi
Hoshiyo	Variation of Hoshi

. . . .

Iku	Nourishing
Ima	Now
Isamu	Rock
Ishi	Stone
Ishie	Dimunitive of Ishi
Ishiko	Variation of Ishi
Ishiyo	Variation of Ishi
Ito	Thread
Iwa	Rock

. . . .

Jin	Tenderness
Jun	Obedient

. . . .

Kaede	Maple leaf
Kagami	Mirror
Kaiyo	Forgiveness
Kama	Sickle
Kameko	Tortoise child (longevity)
Kameyo	Generations of the tortoise
Kane	Of many accomplishments
Kaneru	Bronze
Kaoru	Fragrant
Kata	Worthy
Katsu	Victorious
Kawa	River
Kaya	A yew, or rush
Kazahi	Hair ornament
Kazu	First, or obedient

Kazuko	Variation of Kazu
Kei	Rapture or reverence
Keiko	Variation of Kei
Kichi	Fortunate
Kiku	Chrysanthemum, September flower
Kikue	Chrysantheum branch
Kikuno	Chrysanthemum field
Kimi	Sovereign
Kimiko	Peerless
Kimiyo	Variation of Kimi
Kin	Gold
Kinu	Silk cloth
Kioshi	Clear, bright
Kishi	Beach (longevity)
Kita	North
Kiyo	Pure, happy generations
Ko	Filial piety
Kohana	Little flower
Koko	Stork
Koma	Filly (term of endearment)
Kome	Rice
Konomi	Nuts
Koto	Harp
Kozakura	Little cherry tree
Kozue	Branches of a tree
Kumi	Braid
Kumiko	Braid child
Kuni	Country born
Kuniko	Country-born child
Kura	Treasure house
Kuri	Chestnut
Kurva	Mulberry tree
Kyoko	Mirror

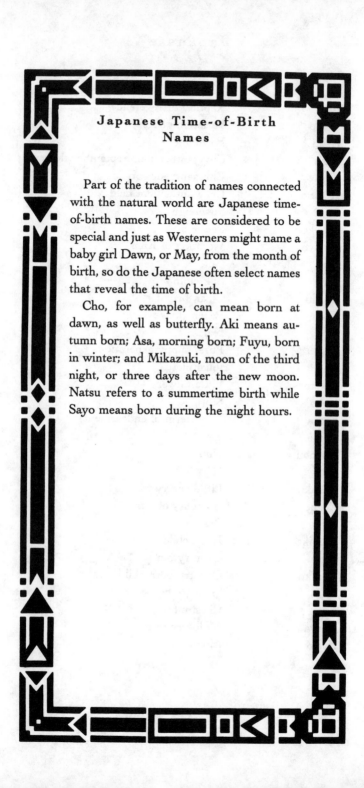

Japanese Time-of-Birth Names

Part of the tradition of names connected with the natural world are Japanese time-of-birth names. These are considered to be special and just as Westerners might name a baby girl Dawn, or May, from the month of birth, so do the Japanese often select names that reveal the time of birth.

Cho, for example, can mean born at dawn, as well as butterfly. Aki means autumn born; Asa, morning born; Fuyu, born in winter; and Mikazuki, moon of the third night, or three days after the new moon. Natsu refers to a summertime birth while Sayo means born during the night hours.

• •

Machi	Ten thousand (good omen)
Mai	Brightness
Mari	Ball
Masa	Straightforward
Masago	Sand (hope for long life)
Masu	Increase
Matsu	Pine (symbol of old age, January)
Matsuko	Pine tree
Michi	The righteous way
Michiko	Beauty and wisdom
Midori	Green
Mie	Triple branch
Mieko	Bright
Mika	New moon
Mikazuki	Moon of the third night
Miki	Stem of the family tree
Mikie	Main branch
Mina	South
Mineko	Peak or mountain child
Miniami	Variation of Mina
Mio	Triple cord
Misao	Fidelity
Mitsu	Light
Mitsuko	Dimunitive of Mitsu
Miwa	Far seeing
Miwako	Far-seeing child
Miya	Shinto temple
Miyo	Beautiful generations
Miyoko	Beautiful generations child
Miyuki	Deep snow (peaceful silence)
Moanna	Ocean
Mon	Gate

Morie	Bay
Mura	Village (coming from a)
Murasaki	Purple

....

Nagisa	Shore
Nami	Wave
Namiko	Variation of Nami
Nani	Beautiful
Naoki	Straight tree
Nara	Oak (sacred tree, stability)
Nari	Thunderpeal
Nariko	Thunder child
Natsu	Born in summertime
Nishi	West (fruit or fruitful)
Nori	Precept, doctrine
Nyoko	Gem or treasure

....

Oki	Middle of the ocean (born at sea)
Oliana	Oleander
Orino	Weaver's field
Ori	Variation of Orino
Osen	Thousand (magical power)

....

Rai	Trust
Raku	Pleasure
Ran	Purity
Rei	Propriety
Reiko	Variation of Rei
Ren	Water lily or lotus (purity)
Riku	Land
Rin	Park (place name)

Roku	Emolument
Ruri	Emerald (protected from evil)
Ruriko	Variation of Ruri
Ryo	Dragon
Ryu	Lofty

• •

Sachi	Bliss
Sada	Chaste
Sai	Talented
Sakae	Prosperity
Saki	Cape
Sakura	Cherry blossom (wealth)
Sato	Sugar
Sawa	Marsh
Sayo	Born at night
Sei	Force, truth
Seiko	Variation of Sei
Seki	Great, barrier or stone
Sen	Wood fairy
Setsu	Fidelity
Setsuko	Variation of Setsu
Shiho	To maintain original intention
Shihobu	Perseverance
Shika	Deer or gentleness
Shina	Possessions, virtue
Shino	Slender bamboo (fidelity)
Shizu	Quiet, clear
Shizue	Variation of Shizu
Shizuka	Variation of Shizu
Shizuko	Variation of Shizu
Shizuyo	Variation of Shizu
Sugi	Cedar (moral rectitude)
Suki	Beloved

Sumi	Refined
Sute	Orphan or foundling
Suzu	Little bell
Suzue	Branch of little bells
Suzuki	Bell tree
Suzuko	Bell child

. . . .

Taka	Honorable, or falcon
Takara	Treasure, precious object
Take	Bamboo
Takeko	Variation of Take
Taki	Waterfall
Tama	Jewel
Tamaki	Bracelet
Tamako	Variation of Tamaki
Tamayo	Variation of Tamaki
Tame	Unselfish
Tami	People
Tamika	Literally, people child
Tamike	Variation of Tamika
Tamiko	Variation of Tamika
Tamiyo	Variation of Tamika
Tanaka	Dweller in a rice field
Tane	Seed
Tani	Valley
Taru	Cask, barrel
Tatsu	Dragon
Tazu	Rice-field stork
Tetsu	Iron (magical protection)
Toki	Time of opportunity
Tokiwa	Everlasting constancy
Tomi	Riches
Tomiju	Wealth and longevity

Tomo	Intelligence
Tora	Tiger
Tori	Bird
Toshi	Year of plenty
Toshiko	Variation of Toshi
Tsuhgi	Second child
Tsuna	Bond
Tsuru	Stork (hope for long life)

. . . .

Umeko	Plum blossom child
Umeno	Plum-tree field
Umeyo	Variation of Umeko
Urano	Coast
Uta	Poem
Utako	Poetry
Utano	Song field

. . . .

Wakana	Plant name

. . . .

Yachi	Eight thousand (good luck)
Yachiko	Variation of Yachi
Yachiyo	Variation of Yachi
Yasu	Peaceful, tranquil
Yasuko	Variation of Yasu
Yasuyo	Variation of Yasu
Yayoi	Spring born (March)
Yoi	Born in the evening
Yoko	Ocean child (female principle)
Yone	Wealth
Yori	Trustworthy
Yoshi	Good, respectful

Yoshie	Dimunitive of Yoshi
Yoshiko	Variation of Yoshi
Yoshino	Fertile field
Yoshiyo	Variation of Yoshi
Yuki	Snow (lucky)
Yukie	Diminitive of Yuki
Yukiko	Snow child (December born)
Yuri	Lily
Yuriko	Variation of Yuri

JAPANESE

Male

Name	Meaning
Akako	Red, a charm to cure disease
Akemi	Beauty of dawn
Akihiko	Bright child
Akio	Bright boy
Akira	Variation of Akio

. . . .

Name	Meaning
Bakin	Literary figure
Bakusui	Literary figure
Basho	Literary figure
Bishamon	Historical figure
Bokusui	Literary figure
Bokuyo	Literary figure
Botan	Peony (flower of June)

. . . .

Name	Meaning
Chika	Near, close
Chikaaki	Variation of Chika
Chikafusa	Variation of Chika
Chikamasa	Close, good
Chikao	Clever, wise
Chishin	Historical figure
Chitose	Thousand years

. . . .

Name	Meaning
Dai	Great

Daigoro	Great fifth-born son
Daijiro	Great second son
Daishiro	Great fourth-born son
Daitaro	Great first-born son
Den	Bequest from ancestors
Denbei	Variation of Den
Dengyo	Historical figure
Denji	Dimunitive of Den
Denjiro	Good ancestors
Doami	Literary figure
Doho	Literary figure
Doni	Historical figure

· ·

Gen	Spring or source
Gendo	Literary figure
Genji	Literary figure
Genjiro	Good source
Genkei	Source of reverence
Genkichi	Fortunate source
Genku	Literary figure
Genmei	Historical figure
Ginjiro	Good silver
Gokomatsu	Historical figure
Goro	Fifth born

· ·

Hajin	Literary figure
Hama	Shore
Haru	Spring born
Haruakira	Variation of Haru
Haruchika	Variation of Haru
Harue	Springtime bay
Harujiro	Spring-born second son

Haruka	Tranquil
Hideaki	Wise or clever
Hiromasa	Broad-minded
Hiroshi	Generous
Hisoka	Secretive, reserved

. . . .

Ietaka	Literary figure
Ike	Literary figure
Iku	Nourishing
Isamu	Rock
Isas	Meritorious one
Ishi	Stone
Ishio	Variation of Ishi

. . . .

Jien	Literary figure
Jiro	Second son
Jo	God will increase
Joji	Farmer
Jun	Obedient

. . . .

Kane	Accomplished
Kazu	First, obedient
Kazujiro	Obedient second son
Kazuo	Man of peace
Ken	One's own kind
Kin	Golden
Kinjiro	Golden second son
Kinshiro	Golden fourth-born son
Kintaro	Golden boy
Kiosho	Clear, bright
Kiyoshi	Quiet, Oriental virtue

Japanese Animal Names

Animal names are common to many cultures. Parents hope the child will evidence the traits of the animal whose name is chosen. Some examples of the Japanese use of animal names are as follows:

Kameko: tortoise or tortoise child
Koko: stork
Tatsu: dragon
Tazu: rice-field stock
Tora: tiger
Tori: bird
Washi: eagle

• •

Makoto	Sincerity
Masahiro	Broad-minded
Masajiro	Good second son
Masajun	Good, obedient
Masataro	Good big boy
Masato	Justice

• •

Naoko	Straight, honest

• •

Raiden	Thunder god
Ringo	Apple (peace be with you)

• •

Saburo	Third-born son
Samuru	His name is God
Sen	Wood fairy (longevity)
Shin	Faithful
Shinakio	Faithful bright boy
Shinjiro	Faithful second son
Shinshiro	Faithful fourth-born son
Shiro	Fourth-born son
Susumu	Literary figure

• •

Tani	Valley
Taro	First-born son or big boy
Tokujiro	Virtuous second son
Tomi	Rich
Toshi	Dimunitive of Toshio
Toshihiro	Wise

Toshio	Year boy

· ·

Yasahiro	Calm, wise
Yasuo	Tranquility
Yemon	Guarding the palace
Yukio	Snow boy, "he goes his own way"
Yoshi	Quiet, tranquil
Yukiko	Variation of Yukio

· ·

Zen	Just
Zenjiro	Just second son
Zenshiro	Just fourth-born son
Zentaro	Just first-born son
Zoami	Artistic figure
Zoki	Literary figure
Zuisho	Literary figure

KOREAN NAMES

There is really no such thing as a common name in the Korean culture. No equivalents to John or Mary exist.

The traditional system is based on generational names, the result of which is that each Korean name is unique. In the generational system, each person is given two names, one of which is also given to all his or her siblings with male or female variation.

For example, the Chung trio of musicians are named, Myung-wha (female), Myung-whun (male), and Kyung-wha (female). These "building-block" names are not always gender specific.

Another example are three daughters named Joo-sun, Sun-joo, and Hei-joo. Two sons of a different family are called Hee-bong and Hee-yong.

Predetermined for generations, the general name is based on the family's surname and a complex cycle related to it. Thus, one family might have a 12-generation cycle of names while another might have a four-generation cycle.

Today, however, partly because of foreign influence, so long kept out of Korea, which was once known as "the Hermit Kingdom," and partly due to smaller families lessening the opportunity to reflect the cyclic name, Korean-Americans tend to choose Anglo-American names for their children or to give them both a Korean name and a Western name.

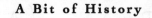

A Bit of History

A mountainous penisula once known as the Hermit Kingdom, Korea remained relatively free of foreign influence until Japan forced the acceptance of a commercial treaty in 1876, opening up Korea to Western influence.

During the first few years of the 20th century, Korean immigrants were recruited as workers in the sugar cane fields of Hawaii. Some 7,000 exchanged passage in return for a work contract of three years. Of these, more than 80 percent remained, many migrating to cities where they set up businesses of their own.

In 1905 the Japanese forced annexation of Korea, in the wake of Japan's victory in the Russo-Japanese War, and abruptly cut off the flow of Korean workers to the United States. However, between 1910 and 1924 approximately 1,000 Korean women were allowed to immigrate as wives for Koreans already there. Known as "picture brides," the men courted them by mail after receiving their photographs and then met them for a dockside marriage so they could legally enter the United States.

Following the Korean War (1950–1953), Korean women and children, as dependents of U.S. servicemen who had been stationed

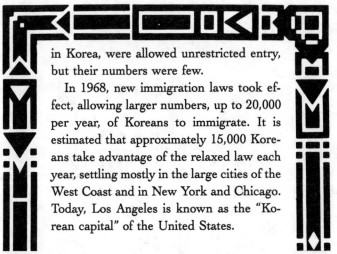

in Korea, were allowed unrestricted entry, but their numbers were few.

In 1968, new immigration laws took effect, allowing larger numbers, up to 20,000 per year, of Koreans to immigrate. It is estimated that approximately 15,000 Koreans take advantage of the relaxed law each year, settling mostly in the large cities of the West Coast and in New York and Chicago. Today, Los Angeles is known as the "Korean capital" of the United States.

Note: Koreans are always given two names one of which is predetermined. The *second* name indicates gender. Although many of the names presented here can be used for both boys and girls, this list provides those names with qualities most usually, though not always, associated with males or females.

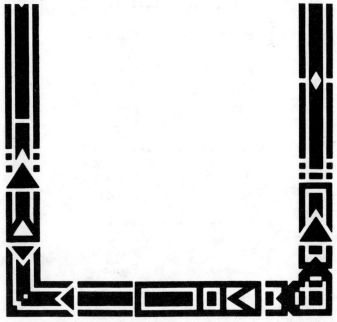

$\mathscr{K}$OREAN

Female

Name	Meaning
Cho	Beautiful
Chun	Justice

. . . .

Name	Meaning
Dae	Greatness

. . . .

Name	Meaning
Eui	Meanings
Eun	Silver

. . . .

Name	Meaning
Hea	Grace
Hee	Pleasure
Hei	Grace
Hye	Graceful
Hyo	Dutiful
Hyun	Wise

. . . .

Name	Meaning
Il	Superior
Ijn	Jewel

. . . .

Name	Meaning
Joo	Precious
Jung	Righteous

. . . .

Kyong	**Bright**

. . . .

Mee	**Beautiful**
Min	**Clever**
Moon	**Literate**

. . . .

Nam	**South**

. . . .

Ryung	**Bright**

. . . .

Shik	**Fertile**
Shin	**Belief**
So	**Smile**
Soo	**Excellent**
Sook	**Pure**
Sun	**Goodness**

. . . .

Yeo	**Mild**
Yon	**Lotus**
Yong	**Face**
Young	**Flower**

$\mathscr{K}$OREAN

Male

Name	Meaning
Bae	Inspired
Bong	Eminent

. . . .

Chin	Precious
Chul	Firm

. . . .

Dae	Great
Doh	Accomplished
Done	Singular
Du	Leader

. . . .

Gi	Brave
Goo	Complete

. . . .

Hee	Bright
Ho	Goodness
Hyun	Wise

. . . .

Ja	Attractive
Jin	Truth

Jung	Righteous

....

Ki	Vigorous
Kwan	Strong
Kyu	Model

....

Myung	Brilliant

....

Sam	Successful
Sang	Helpful to others
Seung	Winner
Soo	Long-lived
Sook	Light
Suk	Hard, firm

....

U	Gentle

....

Whan	Large or enlarging
Woong	Magnificent

....

Yong	Brave

VIETNAMESE NAMES

Many Vietnamese names are traits, which parents believe they can instill in their children by giving them the appropriate names. Ai means beloved or gentle; Cam, to be sweet as an orange fruit; Hanh, faithful; and Trinh, virgin.

Like the Koreans, the Vietnamese do not have common names and create names for each individual child according to the life desired for him and the parent's own philosophy.

Most names are either taken from nature or celebrate moral values such as those most prized by Vietnamese—a respectful attitude towards parents and family, trustworthiness, faithfulness, virtue, and hard work.

Vietnamese pronunciation is subtle, relying heavily on dipthongs. Most of these sounds have no equivalent in English and pronunciation can be only approximate.

$\mathscr{V}$IETNAMESE

Female

Name	Meaning
Ai	Beloved, gentle
Am	Lunar or female principle
An	Peace, safety, security
Ang	Variation of An

. . . .

Be	Doll
Bian	To be hidden or secretive
Bich	Jade, jewelry
Bua	Amulet

. . . .

Cai	Female
Cam	Orange fruit, or to be sweet
Cara	Diamond or precious jewel

. . . .

Ha	River
Hang	Angel in the full moon
Hanh	Faithful, moral
Hoa	Flower, peace
Hong	Pink
Hooang	Gold
Hue	Old-fashioned
Huong	Flower

Hyunh	Yellow

....

Kim	Needle

....

Lan	Flower name
Le	Pear

....

Mieu	Salt

....

Tam	Heart
Thanh	Brilliant
Thao	Courteous (toward parents)
The	Promised
Thu	Autumn
Thuy	Gentle
Ti	Common middle name
Trang	Serious, intelligent
Trinh	Virgin
Truc	Wish
Tuyet	Snow

Vietnamese

Male

Name	Meaning
An	Peace or safety
Anh	Brother
Antoan	Safe or secure

Bay	Seventh-born child
Binh	Peace
Buu	Guide

Cadao	Folk song or ballad
Cham	Hard worker
Chim	Bird

Dan	Yes
Din	Settle down
Duck	Moral
Duy	Virtuous

Gan	To be near

....

Hai	Sea
Han	Sea
Hieu	Respectful
Hoang	Finished
Hoc	Study
Hung	Spirit of a hero or brave
Hy	Hope

....

Kim	Gold or metal

....

Lap	Independent
Long	Hair

....

Ngai	Herb
Ngu	Sleep

....

Pin	Faithful boy

....

Son	Mountain

....

Tai	Talent

HINDU NAMES

There are literally thousands of Indian names which come from the Sanskrit, Hindi, and Gujarati languages. Indians believe that the name a person receives is one of the most precious gifts of a lifetime. They believe the name plays a vital role in shaping the child's life, remaining a good or evil influence forever.

A problem for the use of Indian names in the West is that many of them translate to a negative-sounding pronunciation. Anal, for example, expresses an awkward connotation. Ideally, therefore, an Indian name for a person in a Western culture should be easy to pronounce and have an unambiguous meaning.

As the same Indian name can be spelled more than one way, this listing provides the English equivalent of the Sanskrit spelling.

In addition to the basic name, many suffixes are available with the result that variations of one name are almost endless. For example, Kali combined with das becomes Kalidas, worshipper of Kali.

In a land saturated with religion—manifestations of the various Hindu gods and goddesses are almost countless—it is no surprise that many children receive names of religious significance.

Not only are children named after the plethora of divinities, names are also taken from the great Indian epic *Mahabharata*.

Natural beauties abound in India, a land of many exotic flora and fauna, and girls are often named accordingly.

Other popular names come from rivers, trees, and stars. Occasionally, like some Chinese and Africans, Indians will bestow an ugly name on a child, to protect him from demons. The idea is to trick the demon into thinking the parents place little value on the child.

Most Indian names, however, are both beautiful and of uplifting or attractive meaning.

Hindu Indian

Female

Name	Meaning
Abha	Light, lustrous beauty
Aditi	The earth mother
Ajeya	Unconquerable
Almas	Diamond
Amee	Nectar of immortality
Anita	Grace
Anuva	Knowledge
Ashni	Flash of lightning
Atasi	A blue flower
Atulaa	Incomparable

. . . .

Bahaar	Spring
Bahula	A star, plenty
Bela	Flower
Bhaktajaa	Born out of devotion
Bhamini	Beautiful woman
Bhanumati	Lustrous like sunshine
Bhuma	Earth
Bina	Intelligent
Bodhika	Giver of knowledge
Bulbuli	A songbird

. . . .

Chahna	Love, light
Chameli	Jasmine, or fragrant flower

Chandrani	Wife or queen of the moon
Chandrimaa	Moonlight
Charu	Beautiful
Charulata	A beautiful vine
Chetna	Awareness, consciousness
Chintani	One who likes meditation
Chitkala	Knowledge
Chitrinee	Endowed with many talents

• •

Darsha	To perceive (seer)
Dayita	Beloved (wife)
Devaki	Mother of Krishna
Devangi	One with god-like limbs
Devi	Goddess
Dhairya	Patience
Dhavala	Pure white
Diti	Wife of sage Kashyap
Dularee	Beloved daughter
Durga	Goddess

• •

Edha	Prosperity
Ekavali	Single-string necklace
Ekshuka	Sugar cane
Ela	Cardamon tree (intelligence)
Elaxi	Woman with bright eyes
Elina	Wise woman
Enakshi	Doe eyes
Ershika	Having strong desire
Esha	Wealth, desire, pleasure
Evita	The first woman (Eve)

. . . .

Fagni	Born in the springtime
Falgun	Name of month that brings spring
Forum	Fragrant
Fulki	Spark
Fulande	Made from flowers
Fulangi	Having the body of a flower

. . . .

Ganga	Sacred river of India
Gauhar	Pearl
Gauri	A fair woman, a name of Parvati
Gazal	Song
Geeti	A style of poetry
Girija	Born of a mountain, also Parvati
Gopan	Protected, secret
Goral	Dear, beautiful
Govindi	Devotee of Lord Krishna
Gulab	Rose

. . . .

Haimi	Golden
Hansa	Swan
Harena	Devotee of Lord Shiva
Harita	Green
Harsha	Joy, delight
Hasika	Laughter
Heerak	Bright as a diamond
Heerni	Quick as a doe
Himani	Snow
Hitakshi	One with caring eyes

. . . .

Iha	Wish, desire

Ikshumati	Sweet as sugar cane
Ilakshi	Bright eyes
Ilikaa	Earth
Indira	Goddess Lakshmi
Indrakshee	Beautiful eyes
Indravadhu	Wife of Indra
Induja	Daughter of the moon
Indulekha	Silver crescent (early moon)
Indumati	The full moon

· ·

Jaitun	Evergreen tree
Jalina	One who lives in water
Jambalini	A small water lily
Jasmin	Fragrant flower
Jayaprada	Giver of victory
Jeevankala	Art of life
Jena	Patience
Jharna	A small brook
Jinnat	Heaven
Jowaki	Firefly

· ·

Kali	A bud
Kalpa	Determination
Kanak	Gold
Kanka	Crane or heron
Kanta	Beautiful woman
Kanti	Luster
Kiran	Beam of light
Koman	Delicate
Kujan	Sweet song
Kumud	White lotus that blooms at night
Kunji	Grove of trees

Kunti	Mother of Pandavas

Lajni	Modest, shy
Laksha	White rose
Lakshmi	Name of a goddess
Lalita	Beautiful
Lalna	A beautiful woman
Lasikaa	Dancer
Lata	A beautiful vine
Leena	Devoted
Lekhika	Writer
Lila	Divine play
Loma	Beautiful hair

Mala	Garland
Malka	Queen
Malvi	A musical note
Maya	Illusion
Meena	A precious stone
Meera	Legendary poetess
Meha	Rain
Mita	A friend
Mona	Single, alone, quiet
Moti	Pearl

Neera	Pure
Neeti	Virtuous
Neha	Affectionate, attractive
Nilisha	Blue god
Nimesha	Twinkling of an eye, momentary
Nina	Lovely-eyed

Nishi	Night
Nitya	Eternal (Parvati)
Nivritti	Repose, felicity
Noor	Light

....

Ojal	Vision
Ojasvee	Vitality (force of soul)
Ojasvita	Personality
Ojaswini	An elaborate style
Omana	Woman
Oorjita	Strong, powerful
Oormi	Emotional, flowing

....

Paaru	The sun
Padma	Lotus
Padmi	Lotus goddess
Pakhi	A bird
Panna	Emerald
Parma	Excellent, the best
Prama	Knowledge of truth
Prita	Dear one
Ptali	The trumpet flower
Punam	Day of the full moon
Purna	Complete, fulfilled
Pushpangi	Delicate as a flower

....

Ragi	Single or lover
Ragni	Melody
Reshma	Silky, silken
Reva	Star, the goddess Durga
Riddhi	Prosperity, good fortune

Riju	Innocent
Roshni	Light, brightness
Rujula	Simple, honest
Rupali	Beautiful girl
Rutaja	Daughter of truth

· ·

Sachi	Eloquent, wife of Lord Indra
Sapna	Dream
Sarla	Sincere, honest
Saroj	Lotus
Sejal	River water
Sharda	Goddess of knowledge (Sarasvati)
Smita	Smiling
Sneha	Love, friendship
Sujna	Expert, adept, wise
Syona	Auspicious, happiness

· ·

Tanaya	Daughter
Tanima	Slenderness
Tanvi	Beautiful young woman
Tara	Star, destiny
Tarala	Honeybee (tremulous)
Tarika	Protective, devoted
Tejal	Lustrous, full of light
Timila	A musical instrument
Titali	Butterfly
Tuhina	Snow

· ·

Ujvala	Bright and beautiful
Ulka	Shooting star
Ulupi	Wife of Arjuna

Uma	Goddess Parvata
Urja	Energy (Shakti)
Urmi	Waves of emotion, speed
Urva	The ocean
Urvashi	One who wins your heart
Usha	Dawn
Ushmila	Warm-hearted

. . . .

Vani	Voice, the muse of speech
Vapa	Sowing
Vari	Sea
Venu	Flute
Vidula	Slender like a willow
Vimala	Pure, attractive
Vinita	Modest, unassuming
Vinoda	Full of joy
Virina	Sweet-smelling
Viyati	Bird

. . . .

Yagnya	Sacred fire
Yami	Night
Yamika	Moonlit night
Yamuna	Name of a river
Yashila	Successful
Yashodhana	Rich with fame
Yashodhara	Gautama Buddha's wife, famous
Yogini	Devotee, mediator
Yuti	One who unites
Yuvati	Young girl

Hindu Indian

Male

Name	Meaning
Adil	Sincere, just
Adri	Mountain
Agni	Fire god
Akul	Lord Shiva
Amal	Clean, pure
Amul	Priceless
Anmol	Priceless, precious
Anshu	Sunbeam
Apurv	Unique
Araag	Cool, dispassionate
Asgar	Devotee
Avish	King, earth, ocean

. . . .

Bakul	A flower
Balendra	Lord of lights
Bali	Son of Virochana (god)
Bansi	Flute
Bhanu	The sun
Bhavik	Loving
Bhavya	Elegant, large size
Birjaa	To shine
Brijen	Lord Krishna
Budhil	Learned

. . . .

Chakor	A bird that loves the moon

Chandan	Sandalwood
Chandra	Moon
Chandraraj	King of the moon
Charanjeet	Superior person
Charudatta	Beautiful
Chetan	Life, energy, consciousness
Chintak	Philosophical
Chirayu	Long life
Chitrarath	Chariot of the sun (dazzling)
Chudamani	Crest jewel

· ·

Datta	**O**ne who is given (by God)
Dayal	Compassionate
Dayit	Beloved
Devak	Divine
Dhanesh	King of wealth
Dheer	Patient
Dilawar	Beloved
Dinkar	The sun
Divij	Born in heaven
Dulal	Dear one

· ·

Ehan	**E**xpected
Ehesh	To strive
Ekaagra	One who concentrates
Ekaanta	Solitude
Ekakundala	Lord of the sea
Ekambar	Sky
Ekanath	King
Ekram	Honor
Ekshak	One who sees (visionary)
Eshen	Desirable

. . . .

Falak	Sky, heaven
Falan	Fruitful
Falesh	Lord of fruits
Falgun	Spring (name of first month)
Fanish	King of cobras
Fateh	Success
Firoz	Name of a king
Forum	Fragrant

. . . .

Gagnesh	King of sky
Gajaraj	King of elephant
Garg	Name of an ancient sage
Garuda	King of birds
Girish	King of mountain
Govinda	Lord Krishna
Gulshan	Garden
Gunakara	Endowed with all virtues
Gunratna	A jewel of virtue
Gyandev	Lord of knowledge

. . . .

Hans	Swan
Harikant	Dear to the god
Hariprasad	Blessings of God
Heerak	Bright as a diamond
Hemabh	Covered with gold
Hemant	Early winter (season)
Hilol	Wave of joy
Himal	Snow
Hiral	Lustrous, bright
Hinang	Limbs of henna

. . . .

Ikshan	Visionary
Ikshu	Sugar cane (sweet)
Indeevar	Blue lotus
Indradatta	Given by Indra
Indraneel	Sapphire
Indraroop	Beautiful as Indra
Indrayudh	Weapon of Indra
Iresh	Lord of the earth
Irmaa	The sun
Ishvaku	Lord Rama's family name

. . . .

Jai	Victory
Jalaj	Lotus
Jalal	Glory
Jatilq	Lion
Javed	Immortal
Jayin	Victorious
Jeevesh	Lord of life
Jinendra	Victorious
Johar	Jewel
Jyotirdhar	Holder of the flame

. . . .

Kamlesh	Lord of the lotus
Kanu	Beautiful as Lord Krishna
Kapil	Name of a sage
Karan	Name of a flower
Kaushal	Clever, skillful
Kaushil	Director
Kiran	Ray of light
Kovid	Learned, wise

Kratu	Talented
Kumar	Prince

. . . .

Lahar	A small wave or vibration
Laksh	Aim, goal
Lakshmidas	Devotee of wealth
Lalan	Nurturing
Lalit	Beautiful
Leen	Devoted, absorbed
Lokesh	Lord of the people (Brahma)
Lokpriya	Popular
Lokranjan	Lord Vishnu
Lomesh	Name of a sage

. . . .

Madan	God of love
Mahin	Kingly
Manas	Mind, born from mind
Manik	Ruby
Manil	Name of a beautiful bird
Manu	The first man (Lord Vishnu)
Marut	Wind
Mehul	Cloud or rain
Mihir	The sun
Miraj	Rich, wealthy
Mohal	Attractive
Mohan	Lord Krishna
Mojil	Merry, happy
Motilal	Pearl

. . . .

Nabhi	The best
Nal	A noble king

Nand	Great joy, many achievements
Nara	Supreme spirit, eternal man
Nath	Lord, master, protector
Neel	Sapphire blue
Neh	Affectionate, loving
Nigam	Treasure, the way or path of the Vedas
Nihal	Exalted, happy
Nimai	Filled with inner light
Nuren	Radiance

· ·

Occhave	Festive occasion
Ogaan	Wave
Ojasvi	Vigorous, powerful
Omanand	Joy of OM
Omkar	Sound of OM, the sacred word
Oorjit	Strong

· ·

Paal	Protector
Padma	Lotus
Palak	Twinkling of the eye
Param	The best
Paru	The sun
Patu	Ingenious
Pimal	Fragrance
Piroj	A jewel
Poras	Hero, courageous
Pragy	Wise man

· ·

Rahi	Traveller
Rahul	Gautama Buddha's son

Rajan	King
Rajas	Mastery, fame
Rajiv	A blue lotus
Rajul	Beautiful, decorated
Raka	Day of the full moon
Rasen	One who gives happiness
Rasik	Connoisseur
Ratan	A jewel or precious stone
Ratin	Love and happiness
Ratul	Sweetness
Raven	Excitement and joy
Ravij	Born of the sun
Rishi	A sage or seer
Rushil	Charming
Rutujeet	One who conquers the six seasons

· ·

Saar	Excellent, strong
Sant	An ascetic or devotee
Saral	Honest, simplicity
Sarva	Complete
Satya	Truth, genuineness
Sayam	Evening
Shubh	Auspicious
Shyam	Dark complexion (Krishna)
Sohan	Handsome, charming
Som	Ray of light
Soor	The sun, wise, hero, king
Sthir	Steady, everlasting, faithful
Sujay	Victory
Sunil	Dark blue (sapphire)
Sutap	Good, excellent
Suvir	Courageous

· ·

Taj	Crown
Tanu	Slender
Tanuj	Son
Tapan	Summer
Tejish	Splendor
Toshak	One who pleases
Trigun	The three dimensions
Trupal	Exciting, charming, lively
Tulsidas	Famous saint, author of the Hindi Ramayan
Tungesha	The moon

· ·

Uday	Prosperity, to rise
Udit	Awakened, risen
Udyot	Radiant, lustrous
Ugra	Powerful, fierce
Ujas	Light
Umed	Hope, wish
Upal	Jewel
Urja	Strength, vigor
Urval	Ocean
Utcha	High
Utpal	Lotus
Utsah	Enthusiasm
Uttam	The best
Uttarkumar	An excellent son

· ·

Vajra	Thunderbolt, weapon of Indra
Valak	Childlike, youth
Vanhi	Fire

Vasu	Omnipresent, the sun, good
Vayu	God of wind and air
Ved	A sacred text, sacred knowledge
Venu	Bambo or reed flute
Vinay	One who follows the rules
Vipin	A forest or a garden
Viraj	Resplendent
Viren	Hero, brave
Vivek	Discriminating

· ·

Yaja	A Brahmin
Yakin	Self-confident
Yamal	A pair, or twins
Yash	Glory, fame
Yati	Ascetic
Yograj	Master of yoga
Yuri	Lily
Yuvraj	Heir apparent or prince

*H*ISPANIC *N*AMES

Perhaps more than any other cultural root, Spanish Catholicism spread far and wide into the New World. Not only was Columbus after gold and the fastest route to India, he was also determined to convert the populations of the newly discovered lands to the Catholicism of the pious Queen Isabella. Her husband King Ferdinand, it may be said, wanted gold and knowledge, but his equally determined Queen craved only more and more Catholic subjects.

The fairly brutal conversion of the natives to the religion of Spain left deep marks still visible today in the preponderance of Catholic churches, monastaries, nunneries, and other such appurtenances of Catholicism in all of Latin America. There was no escaping the long arm of the Church, backed up by Spanish militia and fanatic determination.

Thus, Hispanic names, derived from the culture of Spain, Mexico, and other Latin American countries, are typically taken from the Catholic Church's calendar of saints. Both boys and girls are given saints' names.

Not only saints, but martyrs—especially martyred virgins and martyred children—are popular sources for names. Unlike most of the other cultures discussed, which tend toward names often derived from nature, Hispanic names can remind their recipients of sorrow (Dolores or Our Lady of Sorrows), martyrdom (Teresa, the martyred Saint Theresa), or death (Maria de la Cruz or Mary of the Cross).

The Virgin Mary, the mother of Jesus, is by far the most popular source of names for girls, and there are dozens of variations available. Lourdes, for example, the name of one of her most famous shrines, is a common name, as is Guadalupe, the location of another shrine. Maria is the most popular first name of Hispanic girls, existing in countless variations. For example, Maria combines with Flora to create Mariflora; Maria and Linda, Marilinda; Maria and Luz, Mariluz.

Because the Spanish language has changeable endings for nouns to express gender, almost all names are readily convertible from masculine to feminine, and vice versa. Thus, boys can be Mary in the form of Mario, and girls can be called Jesus in the form of Jesusa. The rule applies across the board with few exceptions. Here are some examples:

Masculine Name	*Feminine Name*
Juan	Juanita
Nino	Nina
Rafael	Rafaela
Alejandro	Alejandra

Hispanic names are mostly derived from common European provenance—Juan is a form of John, Alejandro of Alexander, etc. Therefore, they are usually easily recognizable, in their Spanish form, as being derivative of a common name. There are, of course, exceptions, many of these having religious connotations such as Anunciacíon, which refers to a religious festival of the Virgin Mary, Concepcíon, and Immaculata, which refer to her birth, or the Immaculate Conception.

Despite the heavily religious emphasis, there are some names (again, mostly of European origin) which refer to ordinary characteristics. Linda in Spanish means beautiful and there are a dozen forms of Linda—Belinda, Melinda, and so forth. Amapola, also a song title, means a pretty little poppy, and Ginebra refers to white as seafoam, possibly a reference to the "foam-born" Venus.

Sprinkled throughout Hispanic names are those taken from the mythology of the Greeks and Romans, such as Heraclito, Heracles, the Greek hero.

Hispanics are especially fond of "pet" names and a single name can have a dozen variations. Francisco, for example, can be Chico, Paco, Pancho, Curro, or Paquito, to name only a few.

The suffix -cita indicates smallness or little, as Carmencita is "little Carmen."

$\mathcal{H}$ISPANIC

Female

Name	Meaning
Adabella	Lively, lovely
Adina	Delicate
Adriana	Lady of the sea
Africa	Sun
Agripina	Name of saint
Agueda	Name of saint
Albertina	Feminine form of Alberto
Aléjandra	Form of Alexandra
Aléjandrina	Variation of Alejandra
Aleta	Truth
Aletea	Variation of Aleta
Alicia	Noble
Alida	Wing
Alita	Form of Adelaide
Alma	Gentle, refined
Almira	Princess
Aloisia	Form of Eloise
Altea	Knowledgeable, educated
Alvina	Friend to all
Amada	Loved one
Amalia	Industrious
Amanda	Adorable
Amapola	Poppy flower
Amata	Loved
Aminta	Protector, defender
Anda	Going

Andrea	Beautiful
Angelica	Angel
Angelita	Little Angel
Anica	Grace of God
Anita	Form of Hannah
Antonina	Feminine of Anthony
Antuca	Form of Anthony
Anunciacíon	Religious festival of the Virgin Mary
Asela	Slender ash tree
Astra	Like a star
Aurora	Name of saint
Azarias	Child martyr

· ·

Balbina	Name of saint
Basilia	Name of saint
Batilde	Name of queen
Beata	Faithful
Beatriz	Form of Beatrice
Bebe	Baby
Begonia	Name of a flower
Belia	Oath of God
Belica	Form of Belia
Belicia	Form of Belia
Belinda	Graceful
Belita	Diminutive of Belia
Bella	Beautiful (variant of Isabella)
Benedicta	Feminine of Benedict
Benicia	Blessed
Benita	Diminutive of Benicia
Bernardina	Feminine of Bernard
Betina	Form of Betty
Bibiana	Name of saint
Blanca	White (pure)

Bonfilia	Good daughter
Bonita	Pretty, good
Brigida	Form of Bridget
Briseida	Feminine form of Dionysos
Brunilda	Warrior woman

. . . .

Calida	Loving
Camila	Camellia
Candelaria	Illuminateed
Caridad	Name of saint
Carina	Name of saint
Caritina	Name of saint
Carla	Feminine of Carlo
Carlota	Feminine of Charles
Carmen	Crimson
Carmencita	Little Carmen
Casilda	Virgin
Castalia	Pure
Catalina	Form of Catherine
Cecilia	Name of saint
Celestina	Sky or heaven
Chabela	Form of Elizabeth
Chabi	Diminutive of Chabela
Chalina	Latin for rose
Chara	Form of Chalina
Charita	Diminutive of Chara
Chela	Blind
Chica	From Francis
Chila	From Francis
Chiquita	Little one
Chofa	From Sophia
Chofi	From Sophia
Christiana	Feminine of Christ

Christina	After Christ
Chuminia	Lord
Cintia	Goddess of the moon
Citlalia	Star
Clareta	Form of Clara
Clarisa	Form of Clara
Clarita	Diminutive of Clarisa
Clelia	Glorious, sublime
Clio	Famous
Clorinda	Daughter of the leader
Concepcion	Refers to the birth of the Virgin
Conchita	Diminutive of Concepcion
Constancia	Faithful
Constanza	Faithful
Consuela	Adviso, counsellor
Cordelia	Feminine virtue
Corina	Name of saint
Cristy	Annointed

· ·

Dalia	From the valley
Dalila	Delicate
Damita	A little noble lady
Daniela	Feminine of Daniel
Daria	Name of saint
Dea	Feminine of God
Deifilia	Daughter of God
Delfina	Feminine of Delfino, a bishop
Demetria	Form of Demeter, or the name of saint
Dimpna	Name of saint
Dinorah	Light
Divina	Refers to divine providence
Dolorcitas	Diminutive of Dolores

Dolores	Name of Virgin of Sorrows
Doloritas	Variation of Dolores
Dominga	Name of saint
Domitila	Name of saint
Dora	Diminutive of Dorotea
Doris	Goddess of the sea
Dorotea	Name of saint
Dulce	Refers to the names of Mary

. . . .

Edelmira	Form of Adelle
Edita	Form of Edith
Edna	Rejuvenating
Eglantina	Wood rose
Elda	Form of Hilda
Elena	Form of Helen
Eleonora	Form of Elena
Eleuteria	Goddess of freedom
Elisa	Form of Elizabeth
Elsa	Diminutive of Eliza
Elvia	Yellow
Elvira	Spanish place name
Engracia	Form of Grace
Enriqueta	Feminine of Enrique (Henry)
Erendira	Name of a Mexican princess
Erica	Feminine of Erico
Esmeralda	Brilliant, emerald
Esperanza	Hope
Estanislao	From Stanislaus
Estefania	Crown
Estrella	Star
Etelvina	Friend of the nobility
Evelia	Luminous

Evelina	Variant of Eva
Evita	Little Eve

. . . .

Fabiola	Feminine of Fabio
Fanny	Form of Francis
Fausta	Name of saint
Febe	Resplendent
Febronia	Name of saint
Felicia	Faithful
Feliciana	Combination of Felicia and Ann
Felipa	Feminine of Phillip
Filipa	Name of saint
Filis	Form of Phyllis
Filomela	Lover of song
Filomena	Name of saint
Fina	Diminutive of Josefina
Flora	Flower, name of saint
Florenica	From the flowers
Florida	Name of saint
Florina	Name of saint
Fortunata	Name of saint martyr
Fotina	A samaratan
Francisca	Feminine of Francis
Frida	Name of saint

. . . .

Galatea	White as milk
Gardenia	Name of flower
Gaudencia	Name of saint
Gemma	Precious
Generosa	Name of saint
Genoveva	Form of Genevieve
Georgina	Feminine of George

Geraldina	Feminine of Geraldo
Gerda	Protege
Gianina	God has been gracious
Gidita	Strength
Gilda	Form of Hilda
Gina	Form of George
Ginata	From Virgil
Ginebra	White as seafoam
Gisela	Queen
Gitana	Gypsy girl
Gladis	Form of Claudia
Glafira	Name of saint
Glenda	Fertile valley
Gloria	Famous
Glorina	Combination of Gloria and Anna
Gracia	Grace
Graciana	Combination of Grace and Ann
Graciela	Graceful
Greta	Diminutive of Margarita
Griselda	Heroine
Guadalupe	Refers to the Virgin of Guadalupe
Guilla	Form of Julia
Guillerma	Feminine of William

• •

Hada	Destiny
Haide	Variation of Heidi
Henedina	Sweet, agreeable
Herlinda	Name of saint
Hermelinda	Name of saint
Hermina	Feminine of Hermino, a bishop
Hesperia	Tardy
Hida	Variation of Hilda
Hilaria	Name of saint

| Hildegarda | Name of a queen |
| Hipolita | Feminine of Hipolito |

. . . .

Idalia	Sun
Idelia	Noble
Ifigenia	Name of saint
Ileana	Variation of Elena
Illona	Variation of Elena
Imperia	Haughty
Inesita	Little Inez
Inez	Pure or chaste
Ingrid	Daughter
Inocencia	Name of saint
Irais	Name of saint
Irenea	Peace
Iris	Name of a flower
Isa	Variation of Luisa
Isabela	Form of Isabel
Isabelita	Diminutive of Isabel
Isadora	Form of Isis
Isaura	Feminine of Isauro
Isolda	Warrior maiden
Isolina	Diminutive of Isolda
Ivonne	Variation of Yvonne

. . . .

Jacinda	Hyacinth
Jacinta	Name of saint
Jada	Jade
Jandina	Defender of men
Jaquelina	Name of saint
Jazmin	Fragrant flower
Jessica	In God's grace

Jesua	Feminine of Jesus
Jimina	Feminine of Simeon
Joaquina	Feminine of Joaquin
Jocelyn	Beautiful
Jorgina	Feminine of Jorge
Joseé	God will add
Josefa	Feminine of Jose
Joyce	Frank, simple
Joyita	Joy
Juana	Feminine of Juan
Juanita	Diminutive of Juana
Julieta	Downy
Julita	Name of saint
Junita	Form of John
Justina	Name of saint

. . . .

Kika	Home ruler

. . . .

Laureana	Form of Laura
Laurencia	Feminine of Laurencio
Lavinia	Roman wife
Leda	Woman
Lelia	Night
Lena	Diminutive of Magdalena
Leona	Feminine of Leon
Leonilda	That which comes from strife or struggle
Leonor	Shining one
Leticia	Quick, lively
Leya	Loyal to the law
Lia	Languid, restful
Liana	Variation of Juliana

Licha	Noble
Lici	Diminutive of Licha
Licia	Variation of Lucia
Ligia	Melodic
Lilia	Lily
Liliosa	Ninth century martyr
Linda	Beautiful
Liseta	Form of Elizabeth
Lita	Variation of Margarita
Livia	The color olive
Lola	Diminutive of Dolores
Lolita	Sorrow, from Dolores
Loreta	Shrine of the Virgin Mary
Lourdes	Shrine of the Virgin Mary
Lucelia	Combination of Luz and Cecilia
Lucera	That which comes from light
Lucila	Light
Lucina	Light
Lucinda	Variation of Lucina
Lucita	Little light
Lugarda	Name of saint
Luisa	Form of Louise
Luminosa	Name of the Virgin of Lights
Luz	Light, "Maria de la Luz"

· ·

Magaly	From Magdalen
Magda	From Magdalen
Magola	Variation of Magda
Maita	Lady or mistress of the house
Manuela	God is with us
Marcela	Name of saint
Marcelina	Diminutive of Marcela
Marcia	Name of saint

Marcial	Variation of Marcia
Marciana	Combination of Marcia and Anna
Margara	From Margaret
Margarita	Diminutive of Margara
Margarite	Variation of Margara
Mari	Abbreviation of Maria, used in combination names
Maria	The Virgin Mary
Mariluz	Combination of Maria and Luz
Marisa	Contraction of Maria Luisa
Marisol	Contraction of Maria del Sol
Mariquita	From Miriam
Marita	Wished-for child
Maritere	Contraction of Maria Teresa
Martina	From Martha
Maruca	From Miriam
Maruja	Variation of Maruca
Matilde	From Matilda
Matusha	Variation of Matilde
Matuxa	Diminutive of Matilde
Maya	The mother
Medea	Pensive
Mega	Peaceful, gentle, mild
Melba	Wealthy
Melibea	Waters of gold
Melinda	Singer of love songs
Melisa	Honeyed or honeybee
Melisenda	Strong
Melosa	Sweet like honey
Melvina	Sweet lady
Mema	Industrious
Mercedes	Liberator
Milena	Variation of Magdalena
Minerva	Goddess of wisdom

Mira	Marvellous or admirable
Miranda	Marvellous, admirable
Miren	Variation of Maria
Mireya	Name of a poet
Miriam	Hebrew form of Maria
Mirna	Sad, sorrowing
Mirza	A lady
Mitzi	Variation of Maria
Mona	Noblewoman
Monica	Lover of the sun
Mora	Little blueberry
Morena	Form of Miriam

• •

Nadia	Variation of Esperanza
Nadina	Diminutive of Nadia
Nana	Grace of God
Narda	Joyful
Natacha	From Natalia
Natividad	Refers to the birth of Jesus
Necha	Pure or chaste, from Agnes
Nelia	A horn
Neneca	Industrious, striving
Nereida	Water nymph
Nesha	From Agnes
Neva	Snow
Nidia	Nester
Nina	Name of saint
Ninfa	Virgin martyr
Ninita	Little girl
Ninon	Variation of Anna
Nita	From Hannah
Noemi	Agreeable
Nora	Diminutive of Leonora

Noralma	Combination of Nora and Alma
Norma	Feminine form of Norman
Nuela	From Amelia
Nunila	Virgin
Nuria	Shrine of the Virgin Mary

. . . .

Obdulia	Name of saint
Octavia	Feminine of Octavion
Odelia	Name of saint
Odilia	Variation of Odelia
Ofelia	Name of saint
Olga	Sublime
Olalla	Variation of Eulalia
Olimpia	Festival, sky
Olinda	Protectoress of property
Olivia	Name of a plant (olive tree)
Ondina	Water sprite
Orquidea	Name of a flower
Otilla	Name of saint

. . . .

Paca	Dimunitive of Francisca
Paladia	Name of saint
Palma	Palm
Palmira	City of palms
Paloma	Dove or pigeon
Pamela	Singer
Pancha	Nickname for Francisca
Panchita	Diminutive of Pancha
Pandora	Mythological name
Paquita	Diminutive of Pancha
Pastora	Feminine of Pastor
Paulina	Name of saint

Paulita	Little Paulina
Paz	Shrine of the Virgin Mary
Pepita	God will add
Perla	Precious, exquisite
Perpetua	Name of saint
Petronila	Name of saint
Pia	Mystical
Piedad	Shrine of the Virgin Mary
Pilar	Shrine of the Virgin Mary
Pita	Variation of Guadalupe
Pomona	Fertile
Pomposa	Name of saint
Prudencia	Practical, prudent
Purificacion	Pure, sinless

· ·

Querida	Beloved
Queta	Form of Henry

· ·

Rafaela	Feminine of Rafael
Ramona	Feminine of Ramon
Raquel	Form of Rachel
Regina	Queen
Reina	Name of saint martyr
Renata	Feminine of Renato
Ria	River
Rita	Diminutive of Margarita
Rosa	Rose
Rosalba	White rose
Rosalia	Name of saint
Rosalinda	Beautiful rose
Rosamunda	Protector of the horses
Rosana	Combination of Rosa and Ana

Rosario	Garland of roses
Rosaura	Rose of gold
Rosenda	Feminine of Rosendo
Rosita	Diminutive of Rosa
Roxana	Form of Aurora
Rubi	Red
Ruperta	Feminine of Rupert

• •

Sabina	Name of saint
Sabrina	Princess
Samara	From the city
Sancha	Diminutive of Sanchia
Sanchia	Holy
Sancia	Variation of Sanchia
Sandra	Form of Alejandra
Santana	Saint
Sarita	From Sarah
Saritia	Variation of Sarita
Sefora	Form of Eve
Selenia	Sister of the moon
Selma	Justice
Semiramis	Lady of the doves
Serapia	Name of saint martyr
Serena	Name of saint
Sevilla	From Sybil
Seville	Variation of Sevilla
Shaba	Latin form of rose
Sibila	Oracle
Silenia	Feminine of Sileno
Silvana	Feminine of Silvano
Sofia	Wisdom
Soficita	Little Sofia
Sofronia	Wise, thoughtful

Solana	Sunshine
Soledad	Solitary
Sonia	Variation of Sofia
Suela	Short for Consuela
Suelita	Diminutive of Suela
Sulamita	Complete, perfect

• •

Tabita	Gracious
Talia	Flourishing, blooming
Tamar	Variation of Palmira
Tania	Queen of Hades
Tara	Tower
Tarasia	Queen
Tarsila	Name of saint
Tasia	From Anastasis
Techa	Summer
Teodosia	Name of saint
Teofila	Lover of god
Tere	Diminutive of Teresa
Teresa	Name of saint
Teresita	Diminutive of Teresa
Teté	Form of Teresa
Thelma	Feminine of Telmo
Tia	Aunt
Tiana	Combination of Tia and Ana
Tiara	From Tiera
Ticha	She who makes happy
Timotea	Feminine of Timoteo
Tina	Diminutive of Cristina, Ernestina
Tita	Pearl
Tona	From Anthony
Trella	Child of the stars
Tula	Variation of Gertrudis

• •

Urania	Sky, the firmament
Ursula	Name of martyred saint
Ursulina	Diminutive of Ursula

• •

Valda	Heroine
Valentina	Name of saint
Valeria	Name of saint
Valeriana	Combination of Valeria and Ana
Vania	Graced by God
Vera	Truth
Verda	Spring, fresh, joyful
Verna	Born in springtime
Vesta	Guardian of the sacred fire
Victoriana	From Victoria
Victorina	Diminutive of Victoriana
Violeta	Name of a flower
Virginia	Pure
Viridia	Green
Vitoria	Form of Victoria
Viviana	Little one

• •

Wanda	Marvellous, a wonder
Wilfrida	A friend of peace
Wilma	Variation of Guillermina

• •

Ynesita	Diminuntive of Ynez
Ynez	Form of Agnes
Yoli	Form of Yolande
Ysabel	Form of Isabel

....

Zaida	Abundant
Zaira	From flowers
Zoila	Vitality
Zoraida	Eloquent
Zuleica	Big sister
Zulima	Vigorous

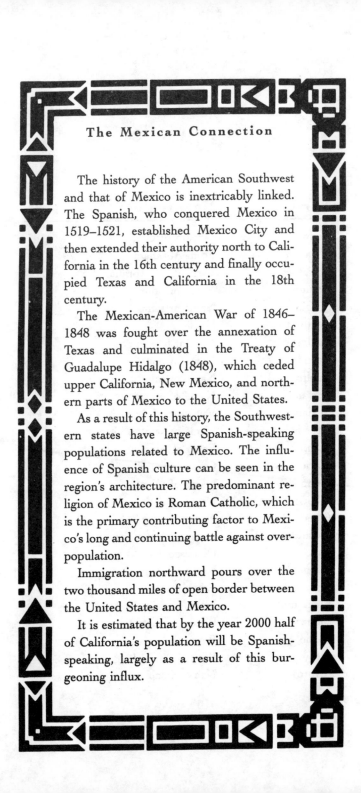

The Mexican Connection

The history of the American Southwest and that of Mexico is inextricably linked. The Spanish, who conquered Mexico in 1519–1521, established Mexico City and then extended their authority north to California in the 16th century and finally occupied Texas and California in the 18th century.

The Mexican-American War of 1846–1848 was fought over the annexation of Texas and culminated in the Treaty of Guadalupe Hidalgo (1848), which ceded upper California, New Mexico, and northern parts of Mexico to the United States.

As a result of this history, the Southwestern states have large Spanish-speaking populations related to Mexico. The influence of Spanish culture can be seen in the region's architecture. The predominant religion of Mexico is Roman Catholic, which is the primary contributing factor to Mexico's long and continuing battle against overpopulation.

Immigration northward pours over the two thousand miles of open border between the United States and Mexico.

It is estimated that by the year 2000 half of California's population will be Spanish-speaking, largely as a result of this burgeoning influx.

$\mathcal{H}$ ISPANIC

Male

Name	Meaning
Abdon	Servant of God
Abrahàn	From Abraham
Abràn	Variation of Abrahàn
Abundio	Name of saint
Acacio	Name of saint
Adelberto	Noble
Adelmo	Ancient helmet
Adeodato	Name of pope
Adolfo	Name of saint
Adrian	Name of pope
Adriano	Variation of Adrian
Agustin	Name of sainted bishop
Alano	Form of Alan
Alarico	Overcoming all
Albano	Name of saint
Alberico	Name of abbot
Alberto	Name of king
Alejandro	Form of Alexander
Alejo	Confessor
Alfonso	Name of saint
Alfredo	Grand
Almaquio	Name of saint
Alonzo	Ready for battle
Alosio	Form of Louis
Alroy	King
Alvaro	Name of saint

Aluino	Form of Alvin
Amado	Lover of the divine
Amando	Variation of Amado
Amato	Loved
Andrés	From Andrew
Antnacio	Name of bishop
Antonio	Name of abbot
Apolinar	Name of bishop
Aquila	Eagle
Arcadio	Name of saint
Archibaldo	Combination of noble and bold
Aristeo	Name of bishop
Arlo	Barberry
Armando	Combination of army and man
Arnulfo	Name of bishop
Arrio	Warlike
Arturo	Form of Arthur
Atalo	Name of abbot
Atenodoro	Name of bishop
Ausencio	Name of bishop
Avelion	From Avella

· ·

Baldomero	Confessor
Baldovino	Intrepid friend
Balta	From Bartholemew
Bardomiano	Name of saint
Barnebas	Apostle
Barto	From Bartholemew
Bartoli	Diminutive of Barto
Bartolo	Solitary
Bartolomé	From Bartholemew
Basilio	From Basil
Baudelio	Victorious

Beltran	Brilliant
Benedicto	From Benedict
Beni	Diminutive of Benedicto
Benitìn	Variation of Benedicto
Benito	Diminutive of Benitin
Benja	Form of Benjamin
Bernabé	Son of consolation
Bernadel	From Bernard
Bernardo	From Bernard
Bertin	Name of abbot
Berto	Diminutive of Alberto
Bertoldo	Variation of Bertin
Blas	From Blaze
Bonfilo	Good son
Bonifacio	Name of saint
Braulio	Name of bishop
Bricio	Name of bishop
Bruno	Name of bishop
Buenaventura	Name of bishop
Bulmaro	Name of abbot

· ·

Cachi	He commands peace
Calixto	Name of pope
Camerino	Name of saint
Canuto	Name of sainted king
Carlo	Form of Carl
Carlos	Variation of Carl
Cashi	From Casimir
Casiano	Name of saint
Casimiro	Name of king
Castel	Castle
Castor	Name of saint
Castulio	Name of saint

Catòn	Wise
Catulo	Wise, subtle
Cecilio	Name of bishop
Celedonio	Name of saint
Celso	Child martyr
Cenobio	Name of bishop
Cenòn	Form of Zeus
Cesareo	Form of Caesar
Chago	Supplanter
Chango	Form of Jacob
Chanti	Diminutive of Chango
Charo	Form of Charles
Che	From Joseph
Checha	Hairy child
Cheche	Diminutive of Che
Chenche	Form of Vincent
Chencho	Crowned with laurel
Chepe	God will add
Chico	Frenchman
Chilo	From Francis
Chipito	Diminutive of Chepe
Chito	Variation of Chilo
Christiano	From Christ
Chumin	Lord
Chuminga	Variation of Chumin
Chumo	Twin
Ciceròn	From Cicero
Ciriaco	Name of saint
Cirilo	Name of bishop
Ciro	Throne
Cisco	From Francisco
Cleme	Variation of Clemente
Clemen	From Clement
Clemente	Name of pope

Clemento	Variation of Clemen
Cleto	Name of pope
Concordio	Child martyr
Conrado	Name of bishop
Constancio	Name of bishop
Cordero	Little lamb
Cornelio	Name of pope
Crescencio	Name of saint
Crisanto	Name of saint
Crisoforo	Name of saint
Crisogono	Name of saint
Crisotomo	Orator, "golden mouth"
Crispo	Name of sainted priest
Cristian	From Christ
Cristino	Diminutive of Christiano
Cristobal	Name of saint
Curcio	From Curtis
Currito	From Francis
Curro	From Francis

· ·

Dagoberto	Name of king
Dalmacio	Name of saint
Damaso	Name of pope
Danilo	From Daniel
Dario	Name of saint
Delfino	Name of bishop
Demetrio	From Demetrius
Desiderio	Name of bishop
Diego	Form of Jacob
Diodoro	Name of saint
Dionis	Of Dionysis
Dionisio	Variation of Dionis
Diosdado	Name of bishop

Domiciano	Name of saint
Domicio	From Dominic
Domingo	Form of Dominic
Donaciano	Name of saint
Donaido	Confessor
Donato	Name of saint

. . . .

Edgar	Defender or "good lance"
Edgardo	Variation of Edgar
Edmundo	Name of sainted king
Eduardo	Name of king
Edvino	Name of king
Efrain	Fruitful, abundant
Egberto	Brilliant, luminous
Eladio	Born in Greece
Eleuterio	Name of sainted pope
Elfego	Name of sainted bishop
Eligio	Name of bishop
Elio	The sun
Eliseo	God is my salvation
Elpidio	Name of saint
Elvio	Yellow, red
Emanuel	Variation of Manuel
Emilio	Form of Emille
Eneas	Praiseworthy
Enrique	Form of Henry
Epifanio	Illustrous
Eracio	Variation of Heracles
Esdras	From Ezra
Estanislao	From Stanislaus
Estéban	Crown
Estevao	From Stephen
Eugenio	From Eugene

Eusebio	Name of saint
Eustaquio	Name of saint
Eustasio	Name of bishop
Eutimo	Name of saint
Eutiquio	Name of pope

• •

Fabriciano	Name of saint
Fabrico	Artisan
Facundo	Name of saint
Farruco	From Francis
Federico	Peaceful ruler
Federoquito	Diminutive of Federico
Fedro	Brilliant, splendid
Felipino	Variation of Filipe
Felo	From Felix
Fernando	From Ferdinand
Fico	Peaceful ruler
Fidel	Faithful
Filipe	Lover of horses
Filipo	Variation of Filipe
Flavio	Blonde
Francisco	From St. Francis
Franco	Variation of Francisco
Frasco	Diminutive of Francisco
Frascuelo	Variation of Francis
Frederico	From Frederick
Fredo	Diminutive of Frederico

• •

Gabino	Name of saint
Galdino	Name of Cardinal
Galeno	Calm, healer
Galo	Name of abbot

Gaspar	Form of Caspar
Gasparcio	Name of bishop
Gencho	Well-born
Generoso	Noble, also martyr
Gerado	From of Gerald, also bishop
Geraldo	Form of Gerald
Gercon	Name of saint
Gerino	Name of saint
Gervasio	Name of saint
Getulio	Name of saint
Gil	Young goat
Gilardo	Name of bishop
Gines	Name of saint
Godofredo	Form of Godfred
Gofredo	Variation of Godofredo
Gontran	Name of king
Gordiano	Form of Gordon, also martyr
Gotardo	Name of Archbishop
Graciano	God's grace, also bishop
Grimoaldo	Name of bishop
Gualberto	Form of Albert
Gualterio	Believer
Guarino	Name of Cardinal
Gudelia	Name of saint
Guido	Woodsman
Guillermo	Form of William
Gustavo	Form of Gustaf
Gutierre	Form of Walter

••

Haraldo	From of Harold, ruler of the army
Hector	Mythological hero
Helio	The sun, Apollo
Heraclido	Form of Heracles

Heraclito	Illustrious, a hero
Herculano	Form of Heracles, martyred bishop
Heriberto	From Herbert
Hermenegildo	Name of saint
Hesiquio	Name of sainted bishop
Higinio	Name of sainted pope
Hilarion	Name of abbot
Homobono	Good man, martyr
Hormisdas	Name of pope
Huberto	Bright mind
Hubi	Diminutive of Huberto
Hugan	Name of abbot

• •

Iban	Form of John
Incenio	Innocent
Indalecio	Name of sainted bishop
Iñigo	Name of abbot
Inocente	Name of pope

• •

Jacinto	Name of saint
Jacobo	Form of Jacob
Jaime	Form of James
Jaimito	Diminutive of Jaime
Jandino	Defender of men
Jando	Variation of Jandino
Javier	Form of James
Jayme	Variation of Jaime
Jenaro	Name of saint
Jeremias	From Jeremiah
Jesus	Savior
Jesualdo	Christian soldier
Joaquin	Form of John

Jobo	Form of Job
Jonas	From Jonah
Jorge	Form of George, farmer
Jorrìn	Farmer
José	Form of Joseph
Josecito	Diminutive of José
Joseito	Variation of Jose
Joselito	Diminutive of Jose
Josue	Form of Joshua
Juan	From John
Juanch	Variation of Juan
Juancho	Diminutive of Juan
Juanito	Diminutive of Juan
Juliàn	Form of Julian
Julio	July
Justino	Form of Justin
Justo	Variation of Justino

· ·

Lando	Diminutive of Orlando
Lao	Camp glory
Laureano	Martyred bishop
Laurencio	From Lawrence
Lazaro	Form of Lazarus
Lencho	Crowned with laurel
Leobardo	Form of Leonard
Leon	Form of Leo, lion
Leonel	Variation of Leon
Leonidas	Family of lions
Leopoldo	Patriot
Liborio	Libertarian
Lico	From Frederick
Lisandro	Liberator
Lope	Wolf

Lorenzo	Form of Laurence
Lucio	Light
Luis	Form of Luis
Lupercio	Name of saint

....

Macedonio	Name of saint
Maclovio	Name of bishop
Macrino	Graceful, slender
Manco	Inca word for king
Mando	From Herman
Mandredo	Valorous
Mango	From Emanuel
Manny	Variation of Mango
Manòlon	From Emanuel
Manue	From Emanuel
Manuel	From Emanuel
Marco	Form of Mark
Marcos	Variation of Marco
Mardonio	Name of saint
Mariano	Pertaining to the sea
Mario	Masculine form of Mary
Martiniano	Form of Martin
Marto	Diminutive of Martiniano
Mateo	From Matthew
Matìas	From Matthew
Mauricio	Name of saint
Maxi	Diminutive of Maximo
Maximiliano	From Maximilian
Maximino	Variation of Maxi
Maximo	Superlative, grand
Mayolo	Name of abbot
Mayorico	Name of saint
Medardo	Powerful, audacious

Melesio	Name of bishop
Meliton	Name of bishop
Melquiades	Name of pope
Metodio	Name of bishop
Micho	Diminutive of Miguel
Miguel	Form of Michael
Migui	Variation of Miguel
Miki	Diminutive of Miguel
Mincho	From Benjamin
Minel	From Emanuel
Mingo	From Dominic
Mique	From Michael
Moctezuma	Pre-Columbian ruler
Modesto	Moderate, temperate
Mondo	The world
Monico	Sun lover
Mucio	Name of sainted priest

· ·

Nabor	Name of saint
Napier	Of the new city
Narcisco	Beautiful
Narno	Name of bishop
Natal	Birthday of the Lord
Natalio	Born during Christmastime
Natan	Gift from God
Nazario	From Nazareth
Necho	From Edward
Nelo	From Daniel
Nemesio	Bringer of justice
Neper	Of the new city
Nereo	Water sprite
Neron	From Nero
Neto	Vigor

Nicandro	Form of Nicolas
Nicanor	From Nicolas
Nicasio	Name of sainted bishop
Nicho	Diminutive of Nicanor
Nicolàs	Form of Nicolas
Nilo	Name of abbot
Noe	Noah
Norman	From the north
Normando	From Norman

• •

Oalo	From Paul
Odiseo	Variation of Ulysses
Olimpo	Near to Mount Olympus
Olo	From Roland
Ordando	From Roland
Orlando	From Roland
Orlo	Diminutive of Orlando
Osmundo	Protector
Osvaldo	Powerful
Otilio	From Otto
Otman	From Otto
Oto	Otto
Otòn	Variation of Oto
Ovidio	Ovid, a Roman poet

• •

Pablo	Form of Paul
Pacifico	Peaceful
Paco	From Francisco
Pacomio	Name of abbot
Pacorro	From Francisco
Paladio	Name of saint
Palmacio	Name of saint

Palmiro	Refers to Palm Sunday
Panchito	Diminutive of Pancho
Pancho	From Francisco
Panfilo	Believer
Pangracio	Child martyr
Pantaleon	Name of a famous doctor
Paquito	From Francisco
Parmeno	Name of saint
Partenio	Name of saint
Partricio	Form of Patrick
Paulino	Form of Paul
Paulo	Form of Paul
Paz	Peace
Pedrìn	From Peter
Pedro	From Peter
Pelagio	Man of the sea
Pepe	From Joseph
Pepillo	From Joseph
Pepin	From Joseph
Pepito	Diminutive of Pepe
Pequin	From Peter
Perequin	From Peter
Pergentino	Child martyr
Perico	From Peter
Petronio	From Peter
Peyo	From Peter
Pio	Name of pope
Pipi	Happy, lucky
Pipo	Variation of Pipi
Piti	Stone, rock
Pitin	From Felix
Pito	From Felix
Placido	Peacemaker

Platòn	From Plato
Prudencio	Practical, careful

. . . .

Quico	Diminutive form, can be applied to many names
Quintilio	Variation of Quinto
Quinto	The fifth
Quiqui	From Henry
Quirico	Name of saint
Quirino	Name of saint
Quito	From Quintin

. . . .

Rafael	God heals
Rafì	Diminutive of Rafael
Raimundo	From Raymond
Ramiro	Name of saint
Ramon	Form of Raymond
Randulfo	Form of Randolph
Raul	Ruler
Raymondo	Variation of Ramon
Raziel	My secret is God
Regino	Masculine form of queen
Remigio	He who knows toil
Renan	Name of philosopher
Reveriano	One who reveres God
Rey	Refers to monarchy
Reynaldo	Form of Reginald
Ricardo	Form of Richard, martyr
Richi	Diminutive of Ricardo
Rico	Variation of Richi
Riel	From Gabriel
Riqui	From Richard

Rober	From Robert
Roberto	Form of Robert, martyr
Robustiano	Name of saint
Rodas	From Rhodes
Rodolfo	From Rudolph
Rodrigo	Ruler
Rodriguez	Variation of Rodrigo
Rogaciano	Name of saint
Rogelio	Form of Roger
Rolando	From Roland
Roldan	Refers to a glorious past
Rollon	From Roland
Rolo	Diminutive of Rollon
Romano	From or near to Rome
Romeo	Character from Shakespeare
Romualdo	Form of Romulus, bishop
Rosalio	Garland of roses
Rubo	Variation of pelirrojo, meaning fair-haired
Rudolfo	Form of Rudolph, child martyr
Rufo	Variation of Rubo
Ruperto	Form of Rupert
Ruy	From Roderick

· ·

Salomon	Peaceful
Salvador	Savior
Sancho	Saint, consecrated to God
Sandro	Variation of Alexander
Sanson	Like the sun
Santiago	Saint
Santo	Sacred, saintly
Sarito	Hairy child
Senon	Living, or given by Zeus

Serapio	Refers to seraphim or angels
Serapion	Variation of Serapio
Severino	Severe, strict, pious
Sidonio	From Sidney
Sigfredo	Variation of Sigfrido
Sigfrido	From Sigfried
Silvano	From the forest
Simplicio	A good and simple man
Sofronio	Thinker
Stancio	Firm and constant (Constantine)

. . . .

Tabo	God's staff
Tacito	He who is called
Tadeo	Praiser, courageous
Tanix	From Stanislaus
Tano	Diminutive of Tanix
Teb	From Stephen
Teodomiro	God's gift
Teodoro	Form of Theodore
Teodosio	Form of Teodoro
Teofilo	God's love
Tiago	From Jacob
Ticho	From Patrick
Tilo	From Stanislaus
Timoteo	From Timothy
Tino	Diminutive of Augustino
Tito	Of the giants
Tobal	Form of Cristobal, Christ-bearer
Tobalito	Diminutive of Tobal
Toli	Farmer
Tomas	Form of Thomas
Tulio	Friend to all
Turi	Diminutive of Arturo

Tuto	From Justin

....

Valdemaro	Brilliant, powerful
Valero	From the fire
Venceslao	Fame and glory
Venturo	Faithful, prestigious
Victoriano	Form of Victor
Viviano	Lively
Vladimiro	Peace and glory
Vulmaro	Warrior

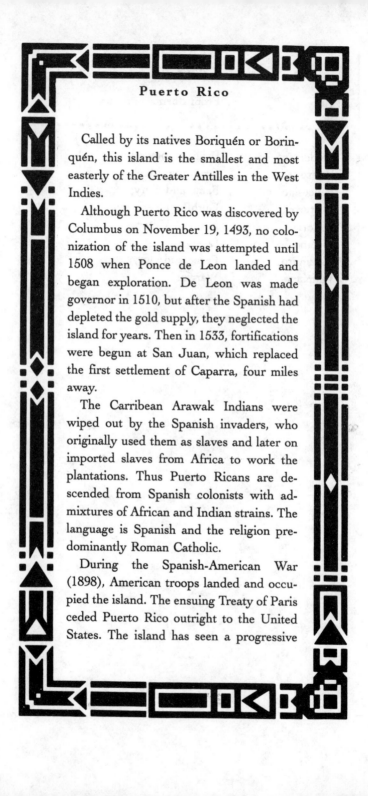

Puerto Rico

Called by its natives Boriquén or Borinquén, this island is the smallest and most easterly of the Greater Antilles in the West Indies.

Although Puerto Rico was discovered by Columbus on November 19, 1493, no colonization of the island was attempted until 1508 when Ponce de Leon landed and began exploration. De Leon was made governor in 1510, but after the Spanish had depleted the gold supply, they neglected the island for years. Then in 1533, fortifications were begun at San Juan, which replaced the first settlement of Caparra, four miles away.

The Carribean Arawak Indians were wiped out by the Spanish invaders, who originally used them as slaves and later on imported slaves from Africa to work the plantations. Thus Puerto Ricans are descended from Spanish colonists with admixtures of African and Indian strains. The language is Spanish and the religion predominantly Roman Catholic.

During the Spanish-American War (1898), American troops landed and occupied the island. The ensuing Treaty of Paris ceded Puerto Rico outright to the United States. The island has seen a progressive development toward self-rule particularly since 1948 when Luis Muñoz Marìn became the first governor elected by the people. Puerto Ricans have U.S. citizenship and therefore freely take up residence in the United States, which boasts a large population of natives from the chronically overpopulated island, concentrating mainly in New York City and other East Coast cities.

Now a commonwealth, the result of a 1967 vote, Puerto Ricans frequently debate the advantages and possibilities of both statehood and total independence.

NATIVE AMERICAN NAMES

Native American populations inhabiting the land before the advent of Europeans were extremely diverse, living many different ways of life from groups of simple food-gatherers to nomadic tribes which followed the herds of buffalo.

These varying styles of life are reflected in the names used by different tribes. Today, there are approximately one million people of Indian or part-Indian ancestry and more than half of them live on reservations across the United States. Of the original Indian "nations," estimated at two hundred, there are still about 170 tribes that maintain their own cultural identities.

Thus, there is no one particular identifiable naming tradition that can be called Native American. In some tribes, conceptual names were passed down through the generations. Walking Bear, for example, might be the grandson of Standing Bear.

Native Americans have a strong belief in the individuality of each person, who is considered to have a unique soul. Therefore, they rarely name a child after a parent but might choose a name reflecting the deeds of a grandparent, or a great-grandparent.

In some tribes, notably the Kiowas, naming a child

after a recently deceased relative was strictly forbidden. On the other hand, some Eskimos believe that it is absolutely necessary to give a newborn the name of a recently deceased relative. In still other tribes, naming a child after a living relative is considered bad luck.

Like the Chinese, Koreans, and Vietnamese, American Indians tend to create new names for each child with the result that there are no most common names.

Typically, names reflect the natural world, and of the nature names, bear names are probably the most frequent, often found among the Miwok of California. Etumu means bear warming itself in the sunlight, while Notaku means growling of a bear as someone passes by. Another favorite of the Miwok, Chicken hawk names, are especially colorful. Consider Noksu or smell of a chicken hawk's nest and Tiwolu, chicken hawk turning its eggs with its bill while they are hatching.

In addition to nature names, magical names associated with religious beliefs and names that mark times of war and peace (the Navajo especially do this) are used.

Names may also refer to a dream one parent had at the time of the child's birth.

Some names contain whole stories. For example, the Miwok name Muliya means *to beat or hit*, but to the person named Muliya his name means Hitting farewell-to-spring seed with a stick as the seed hangs on the bush. The Miwok have a number of these "farewell-to-spring" seed names. The frequency of seed-referring names are indicative of the importance of seeds as a food source and as material for jewelry making.

The complexity hidden behind Indian names does not translate well into English. Where possible in this listing, the tribe of origin for a name is indicated, but as the Indian languages were an oral and not a written tradition, the precise origination of many names is unknown.

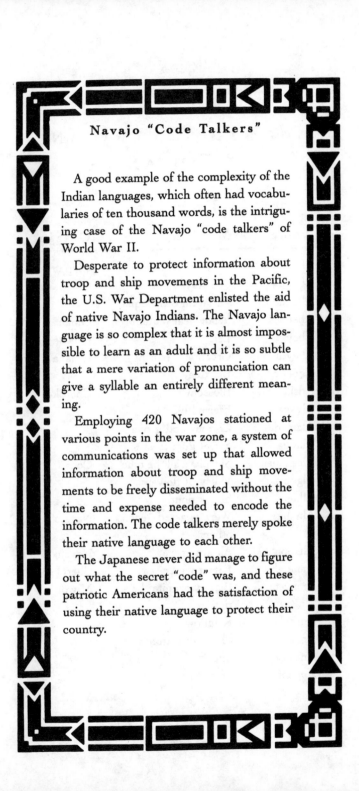

Navajo "Code Talkers"

A good example of the complexity of the Indian languages, which often had vocabularies of ten thousand words, is the intriguing case of the Navajo "code talkers" of World War II.

Desperate to protect information about troop and ship movements in the Pacific, the U.S. War Department enlisted the aid of native Navajo Indians. The Navajo language is so complex that it is almost impossible to learn as an adult and it is so subtle that a mere variation of pronunciation can give a syllable an entirely different meaning.

Employing 420 Navajos stationed at various points in the war zone, a system of communications was set up that allowed information about troop and ship movements to be freely disseminated without the time and expense needed to encode the information. The code talkers merely spoke their native language to each other.

The Japanese never did manage to figure out what the secret "code" was, and these patriotic Americans had the satisfaction of using their native language to protect their country.

NORTH AMERICAN INDIAN

Female

Name	Meaning	Origin
Abedabun	Peep of day (dawn)	Chippewa
Abequa	She stays home	Chippewa
Abeque	Variation of Abequa	
Abetzi	Yellow leaf (autumn)	Omaha
Abey	Leaf	Omaha
Abeytu	Green leaf (spring)	Omaha
Adoette	Big tree	
Adsila	Blossom	Cherokee
Aiyana	Eternal bloom	
Alameda	Cottonwood grove	
Alaqua	Sweet gum tree	
Aleshanee	She plays all the time	Coos
Algoma	Valley of flowers	
Alkas	She is timid	
Alnaba	Wars passed each other	Navajo
Altsoba	All are at war	Navajo
Amadahy	Forest water	Cherokee
Amayeta	Big manzanita berries	Miwok
Amitola	Rainbow	
Anaba	She returns from war	
Anevay	Superior	
Angeni	Spirit angel	

Anpaytoo	Radiant	Sioux
Aponi	Butterfly	Pima
Aquene	Peace	
Atepa	Wigwam	Choctaw
Awanata	Turtle	Miwok
Awenasa	My home	Cherokee
Awendela	Early day (born after dawn)	
Awenita	A fawn	
Ayashe	Little one	Chippewa
Ayita	First in the dance	Cherokee

· ·

Bena	Pheasant
Bly	High (hope for a tall child)

· ·

Chapa	Beaver	Sioux
Chapawee	Industrious	Sioux
Chenoa	White dove (peace in nature)	
Chilali	Snowbird	
Chimalis	Bluebird	
Chitsa	Fair one	
Cholena	Bird	Delaware
Chuma	Rattlesnake girl	Hopi
Chumana	Variation of Chuma	Hopi
Chumani	Dewdrops	Sioux
Cocheta	The unknown	

· ·

Dena	Dale or valley	
Dezba	Going to war	Navajo

Doba	There was no war	Navajo
Doli	Bluebird	Navajo
Donoma	Visible sun	Omaha
Dowanhowee	Singing voice	Sioux
Dyani	A deer	

. . . .

Ehawee	Laughing maid	Sioux
Elu	Beautiful or fair	Zuni
Enola	Alone	
Etenia	Wealthy	
Eyota	The greatest	

. . . .

Fala	Crow	Choctaw
Flo	Like an arrow	

. . . .

Gaho	Mother	
Galilahi	Amiable, attractive	Cherokee

. . . .

Haloke	Salmon	Navajo
Halona	Happy fortune	
Hana	Sky, or black cloud	Arapaho
Hantaywee	Cedar maid (faithful)	Sioux
Hateya	To press with the foot	Miwok
Helki	To touch	Miwok
Heta	Race after a rabbit hunt	Hopi
Hiti	Hyena (totem)	Eskimo
Hola	Ceremonial seed-filled club	Hopi
Honovi	Strong deer	Hopi

Huata	Carrying seeds in a basket	Miwok
Humita	Shelled corn	Hopi
Huyana	Rain falling	Miwok

. . . .

Ilia	Unknown meaning	
Imala	Disciplinarian	
Isi	Deer	Choctaw
Istas	Snow	
Ituha	Sturdy oak	
Iuana	Blowing backward as the wind blows over the waters of a bubbling stream	
Izusa	White stone	

. . . .

Kachina	Sacred dancer	
Kai	Willow tree	Navajo
Kaliska	Coyote chasing deer	Miwok
Kamata	Throwing gambling bones	Miwok
Karmiti	Trees	Eskimo
Kasa	Fur robe (garment)	Hopi
Kaya	My elder sister	Hopi
Keezheekoni	Fire briskly burning	Chippewa
Kimama	Butterfly	Shoshone
Kimimela	Butterfly	Sioux
Kineks	Rosebud	
Kirima	A hill	Banti Eskimo
Kiwidinok	Woman of the wind	Chippewa
Koko	Night	Blackfoot

Koleyna	Fish coughing	Miwok
Kulya	Sugar-pine nuts burned black	Miwok
Kwanita	God is gracious	Zuni

. . . .

Lenmana	Flute girl	Hopi
Leotie	Prairie flower	
Liluye	Chicken hawk singing while soar-ing	Miwok
Liseli	Unknown meaning	Zuni
Lissilma	Be thou there	
Litonya	Hummingbird dart-ing down	Miwok
Lolotea	God's gift	Zuni
Lomasi	Pretty flower	
Lulu	Rabbit	
Luna	Moon	Zuni
Lusela	Bear swinging its foot while licking it	Miwok
Lusita	Bringer of light	Zuni
Luyu	Wild dove	Miwok

. . . .

Macawi	Motherly	Sioux
Macha	Aurora	Sioux
Magaskawee	Sawn maiden (graceful)	Sioux
Magena	The coming moon	
Mahala	Woman	
Mai	Coyote	Sioux
Maka	Earth	Sioux

Makawee	Earth maiden	Sioux
Malia	Bitter (from Mary)	Zuni
Malila	Salmon going fast up a rippling stream	Miwok
Manaba	War returned with her coming	Navajo
Mankalita	Pearl	Zuni
Mansi	Plucked flower	Hopi
Mapiya	Heavenly	Sioux
Maralah	Born at earthquake time	
Masalina	Unknown meaning	Zuni
Mausi	Plucking flowers	
Meda	Prophet	
Meli	Form of Mary	Zuni
Memdi	Henna plant	
Meoquanee	Clothed in red	Chippewa
Meriwa	Thorn	Eskimo
Miakoda	Power of the moon	
Migina	Moon returning (child born at new moon)	Omaha
Migisi	Eagle	Chippewa
Mika	The knowing raccoon	
Mimiteh	New moon	Omaha
Minaku	Berry woman	Blackfoot
Minal	Fruit	
Minowa	Moving voice	
Minya	Elder sister	Minya
Misae	White sun	Osage
Mitena	Born under new moon	Omaha

Mituna	Wrapping a salmon with willow stems and leaves after catching it	Miwok
Mona	Gathering jimson-weed seed	Miwok
Mulya	Knocking acorns off a tree	Miwok
Muna	Born when the streams rise	Hopi

• •

Nahimana	Mystic	Sioux
Namid	Star dancer	Chippewa
Nara	Place name	
Nasan	Surrounded by song	Carrier
Nascha	Owl	Navajo
Nashota	Twin	
Nata	Speaker or creator	
Nata-akon	Expert canoeist	Chippewa
Natane	Daughter	Arapaho
Neka	The wild goose	
Netis	Trusted friend	
Niabi	A fawn	
Nida	Mythical being	Omaha
Nidawi	Fairy girl	Omaha
Nina	Mighty	
Ninita	Little girl	Zuni
Nita	Bear	Choctaw
Nituna	My daughter	
Nolcha	The sun	
Nova	Chasing a butterfly	Hopi
Nuna	Land	

• •

Odahingum	Ripple on the water	Chippewa
Odina	Mountain	Algonquin
Ogin	The wild rose	
Ojinjintka	Queen of flowers (the rose)	Sioux
Olathe	Beautiful	
Ominotago	Pleasant voice	Chippewa
Omusa	To miss with arrows	Miwok
Onatah	Corn spirit (daughter of the earth)	Iroquois
Onawa	Wide-awake one	
Onida	The looked-for one	
Opa	Owl	Choctaw
Orenda	Magical powers	Iroquois
Oya	To name (the jack-snipe)	Miwok

• •

Pakuna	Deer jumping	Miwok
Papina	Vine growing on an oak tree	Miwok
Pati	To break by twisting	Miwok
Pazi	Yellow bird	Ponca
Pelipa	Lover of horses	Zuni
Peni	His mind (communicate with spirits)	Carrier
Peta	Golden eagle	Blackfoot
Poloma	Bow	Choctaw
Posala	Farewell to spring flower	Miwok
Ptaysanwee	White buffalo (queen of the herd)	Sioux

....

| Rozene | A rose | |

....

Sadzi	Sun heart (a clock)	Carrier
Sahkyo	Mink	Navajo
Salali	Squirrel	Cherokee
Sanuye	Red cloud coming (sunset)	Miwok
Sapata	Bear hugging tree	Miwok
Satinka	Magic dancer	
Sedna	The goddess of food	Eskimo
Shada	Pelican	
Shappa	Red thunder (born during a violent storm)	
Sheshebens	Duckling	Chippewa
Shumana	Rattlesnake girl	Hopi
Sihu	Flowering bush	
Sinopa	Kit fox	Blackfoot
Sipeta	To pull out	Miwok
Sisika	Swallow or thrush	
Sitala	Display memory	
Snana	Jingles like little bells	Sioux
Sora	Warbling songbird	
Soso	Tree squirrel biting a tiny hold in a pine nut	Miwok
Sula	Little she-bear	
Suletu	To fly around	Miwok
Suni	A Zuni Indian	Zuni
Sunki	Overtake	Hopi
Suzamni	Graceful lily	Carrier

. . . .

Taci	Washtub	Zuni
Tadewi	Wind	
Tadita	A runner	Omaha
Taima	Crash of thunder	
Taini	Coming new moon	Omaha
Taipa	To spread wings	Miwok
Takala	Corn tassel	Hopi
Takchawee	Doe (gentle or loving)	Sioux
Takenya	Falcon swooping	Miwok
Tala	Wolf (wily intelligence)	
Talasi	Corn tassel flower	Hopi
Talula	Leaping water	Choctaw
Talutah	Scarlet	Sioux
Tama	Thunderbolt	
Tansy	The tansy flower	Hopi
Tasida	Rider (of a horse)	Sarcee
Tateeyopa	Happy hostess	Sioux
Tayanita	Young beaver	Cherokee
Tehya	Precious	
Tiponya	Great horned owl poking egg	Miwok
Tiwa	Onions	Zuni
Tolikna	Coyote's long ears flapping	Miwok
Toski	A squashbug	Hopi
Totsi	Moccasins	Hopi
Tusa	Prairie dog	Zuni
Tuwa	Earth	Hopi

. . . .

Una	**R**emember (coyote)	Hopi

Urika	Useful to all	Omaha
Utina	Woman of my country	

. . . .

Wachiwi	Dancing girl	Sioux
Waitilanni	Wonder water	Laguna
Wakanda	Inner magical power	Sioux
Waneta	The charger	
Wanetta	Little pale one	
Wasula	Little hailstorm (impulsive)	Sioux
Wauna	Snow geese calling as they fly	Miwok
Weeko	Pretty girl	Sioux
Wenona	First-born daughter	
Wicapiwakan	Holy star	Dakota
Wihakayda	Youngest daughter	Sioux
Wihunahe	Chief woman	Cheyenne
Winona	Eldest daughter	Sioux
Witashnahq	Untouched (virgin)	Sioux
Wyanet	Beautiful	

. . . .

Yamka	Flower budding	Hopi
Yanaba	She meets the enemy	Navajo
Yepa	Snow maiden	
Yoki	Bluebird on the mesa	
Yoluta	Fairwell-to-spring seed	
Yoomee	Star	Coos

. . . .

Zaltana	High mountain

Zihna	Spinning	Hopi
Zitkala	Bird	Dakota
Zonta	Trustworthy	Sioux

NORTH AMERICAN INDIAN

Male

Name	Meaning	Origin
Adahy	In the woods	Cherokee
Agnaiyanke	Runs beside the horse	Dakota
Ahanu	He laughs	
Ahdik	Caribou or reindeer	
Ahmik	Beaver (skillful)	
Akando	Ambus (commemorative)	
Akecheta	Warrior	Sioux
Akule	He looks up (alert baby)	
Anoki	Actor	
Apenimon	Trustworthy	
Apiatan	Wooden lance	Kiowa
Awan	Somebody (a personage)	

· ·

Name	Meaning	Origin
Bedagi	Big thunder	Wabanaki
Bemossed	Walker	
Biminak	Slick roper	
Bimisi	Slippery	
Bodaway	Firemaker	

· ·

Chankoowashtay	Good road	Sioux
Chashchunka	Wave	Winnebago
Chayton	Falcon	Sioux
Chesmu	Gritty	
Ciqala	Little	Dakota

· ·

Dasan	Leader of the bird clan
Delsie	Variation of Delsin
Delsin	He is so
Delsy	Variation of Delsin
Dichali	Talkative
Dishaly	Variation of Dichali
Dohosan	Small bluff
Dyami	Eagle

· ·

Elan	Friendly	
Elia	Jehova is God (Spanish)	Zuni
Elki	To hang on the top of	Miwok
Elsu	Flying falcon	
Enapay	Comes out (brave)	Sioux
Enli	That dog over there	Dene
Enyeto	The bear's way of walking	
Etu	The sun	
Ezhno	He goes alone	

· ·

Gomda	Wind

Gosheven	The great leaper	
Guyapi	Candid	

· ·

Hakan	Fiery	
Halian	Youthful	Zuni
Hanee	A beggar	
Helaku	Sunny day	
Helki	To touch	Miwok
Helushka	Warrior	Winnebago
Hesutu	Taking yellow jacket nest	Miwok
Hiamovi	High chief	Cheyenne
Hinto	Blue	Dakota
Hinum	God of clouds and rain	
Hoho	Bear growing	Miwok
Honon	Bear	Miwok
Honovi	Strong	
Hotah	White	Sioux
Hototo	Whistler	
Howahkan	Mysterious voice	Sioux
Howi	Turtle dove	Miwok
Huhusecaska	White bones	Dakota
Hulwema	Dead grizzly shot and killed	Miwok
Huslu	Bear with lots of hair	Miwok
Hute	Star in the Big Dipper	

· ·

Igasho	Wanderer	

Inteus	He shows his face; he is not ashamed	
Istu	Sugar-pine sugar	
Iye	Smoke	

· ·

Jacy	The moon (creator of plants)	Tupi-Guarani
Jolon	Valley of the dead oaks	

· ·

Kaga	Tribe chronicler	
Kangee	Raven	Sioux
Kara	Broken-fingered one	Banti Eskimo
Kele	Sparrow hawk	Hopi
Kelle	Variation of Kele	
Kibbe	The night bird	Nayas
Kijika	He walks quietly	
Knoton	The wind god Nodin	
Kohana	Swift	Sioux
Kono	Tree squirrel biting pine nut	Miwok
Kosumi	Fishing for salmon with a spear	Miwok
Kuruk	Bear	Pawnee
Kuzih	Great talker	Carrier
Kwam	God's gracious gift	Zuni

· ·

Lagundo	Peaceful	
Lan-hononoma	Standing flute	Hopi
Lanu	Refers to tribal custom	Miwok

Len	Flute	Hopi
Lenno	Man	
Lesharo	Chief	Pawnee
Leyati	Shape of abalone shell	Miwok
Lise	Salmon's head coming out of water	Miwok
Liwanu	Bear growling	Miwok
Lokni	Rain coming through a small hole in the roof	Miwok
Lonan	Cloud	Zuni
Lonato	Flint	
Lootah	Red	Sioux
Lusio	Bringer of light	Zuni
Luyu	To shake the head	Miwok

· ·

Mahkah	Earth	Sioux
Mahpee	Sky	Sioux
Makya	Eagle hunter	Hopi
Manipi	A walking wonder	
Maona	Earthmaker (deity)	Winnebago
Maska	Powerful	
Masou	Fire deity	
Mato	Brave	
Matonazin	Standing bear	Dakota
Matoskah	White bear	Sioux
Mazablaska	Piece of flat iron	Dakota
Melvern	Great chief	
Metikla	Reaching underwater to catch white sucker fish	Miwok
Mika	Raccoon	Ponca

Mikasi	Coyote	Omaha
Milap	He gives	
Mingan	Gray wolf	
Misu	Rippling water	Miwok
Mojag	Never quiet (crying baby)	
Molimo	Bear going into tree's shade	Miwok
Momuso	Yellow jackets piled in their winter nest	Miwok
Mona	Gathering jimson-weed seed	Miwok
Motega	New arrow	
Muata	Yellow jackets in the nest	Miwok
Muraco	White moon	

. . . .

Nahele	Forest	
Nahios-si	Three fingers	Cheyenne
Nahma	The sturgeon	
Nakos	Sage	Arapaho
Nalren	He is thawed out	Dene
Namid	Star dancer	Chippewa
Nantai	Chief	Navajo
Nantan	Spokesman	Apache
Napayshni	He does not flee (courage)	Sioux
Nashashuk	Loud thunder	
Nashoba	Wolf	Choctaw
Nawat	Left-handed	
Nawkaw	Wood	
Nayati	Wrestler	
Neka	Wild goose	

Nibaw	I stand up	
Nigan	Ahead	
Nikiti	Round and smooth like an abalone shell	
Nitis	Good friend	
Nodin	The wind	
Notaku	Bear growling at passerby	Miwok

....

Odakota	Friendly	**S**ioux
Ogaleesha	Red shirt	Sioux
Ogima	Chief	Chippewa
Ohanko	Reckless	
Ohanzee	Shadow	Sioux
Ohitekah	Brave	Sioux
Otadan	Plenty	
Otaktay	Strikes many (killer)	
Otu	Sea shells in a basket	
Ouray	Arrow	
Oya	Naming the jack-snipe	Miwok

....

Paco	Bald eagle	
Pallaton	Fighter	
Pat	Fish	
Patakasu	Small ant biting a hand	Miwok
Patamon	Raging	
Patwin	Man (legendary figure)	Litwaito
Payat	He is coming	
Paytah	Fire	Sioux

Pilan	God of thunder, lightning	Araucanian
Pinon	A god who became Orion	
Powan	Rich	

· ·

Quanah	Fragrant	Commanche

· ·

Raini	Creator of the world (god)	Tupi-Guarani

· ·

Sahale	Falcon	
Sakima	King	
Sakuruta	Coming sun	Pawnee
Sewati	Curving of bear claws	Miwok
Siwili	Long tail of the fox	
Skah	White	Sioux
Skiriki	Coyote	Pawnee
Son	Star	
Songan	Strong	

· ·

Tadi	Wind	Omaha
Tadzi	Loon	Carrier
Taima	Thunder (born in a storm)	
Takoda	Friend to many	Sioux
Talli	Legendary hero	
Tapko	Antelope	Kiowa
Tasunke	Horse	Dakota

Tatankaptecila	Short bull	Dakota
Tate	Windy, a talker	
Teetonka	Big lodge	Sioux
Telutci	Bear making dust as it runs	Miwok
Tiimu	Caterpillar	Miwok
Tohan	Cougar	
Tokala	Fox	Dakota
Tooantuh	Spring frog	Cherokee
Tuari	Young eagle	Laguna
Tuketu	Variation of Telutci	Miwok
Tukuli	Caterpillar traveling headfirst down a tree in summertime	Miwok
Tunu	Deer thinking about eating wild onions	Miwok
Tupi	To pull up (a salmon)	Miwok
Tyee	Chief	

• •

Uzumati	Grizzly bear	Miwok

• •

Viho	Chief	Cheyenne

• •

Waban	The east wind	
Wahchinksapa	Wise, clear-headed	Sioux
Wahchintonka	Patient	Sioux
Wahkan	Sacred	Sioux
Wahkoowah	Charging	Sioux
Wakiza	Fighter	
Wamblee	Eagle	Sioux

Wambleeska	White eagle	Sioux
Wambliwaste	Good eagle	
Wanageeska	White spirit	Sioux
Wanahton	Charger	Sioux
Wanmikiya	Savior	Sioux
Wapi	Lucky	
Weayaya	Setting sun	Sioux
Wehinahpay	Rising sun	Sioux
Wemilat	Child born to wealthy parents	
Wemilo	All speak to him (respect)	
Wenutu	Sky clearing after clouds	
Wicasa	Man	Dakota
Wichado	Willing	
Wilanu	Pouring water on acorn flour	Miwok
Wilny	Eagle singing while flying	
Wilu	Chicken hawk calling "wi"	
Wingi	Willing	
Wuliton	To do well	
Wunand	God is good	
Wuyi	Turkey vulture soaring	Miwok
Wynono	First-born son	

....

Yahto	Blue	Sioux
Yakecen	Sky song	
Yakez	Heaven	Carrier
Yancy	Englishman	

Yoskolo	Breaking off pine cones
Yotimo	Yellow jacket carrying food to its nest
Yuma	Son of a chief
Yutu	Coyote making a Miwok feint so he can seize a bird

HAWAIIAN NAMES

Because of the 19th-century invasion of Christian missionaries, today many contemporary Hawaiian names are developments or versions of Biblical or English names. Akela, for example, is a form of Adelle; Akoni, a form of Anthony; Kama, Thelma; Lahela, Rachel; and Malia, Mary.

Sometimes Hawaiians give a child an English first name and a Hawaiian middle name, which produces some interesting combinations, such as Elizabeth Pualani which could be construed to mean a heavenly flower that believes in God as perfection. Another example might be Delores Melei, which would mean sorrowful song child.

The Hawaiian tradition of using names that describe a celestial condition or event may have arisen because that was the first thing the father saw after his child's birth. If, for example, he looked up into the dawn's early light, he might name his daughter Aulaula or if he saw a seagull swoop overhead, she might be named Iwalani, heavenly sea bird.

Another custom is looking upon the child as a gift from God, or heaven. Makana has such a meaning.

Typically, names can be given to either boys or girls so there is no sharp male/female division of names, nor is it possible to determine the sex of a person just by hearing his or her name, somewhat confusing for those used to thinking a person's name is a reliable guide to gender.

The element of creativity is important in Hawaiian names, and a number of root words are used in combination to create new and unique names. Some of these are Lani, sky or heavenly; Ani, beautiful; Ipo, darling; Pua, flower; and Olu, gentle.

Two popular combinations are Pualani, meaning flower of heaven and Iaolani, name of a beautiful star.

With the list given here, you can be as creative as you like in giving your child a beautiful, melodious Hawaiian name, rich with descriptive charm.

A Bit of History

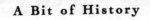

Admitted in 1959 as a the 50th state, Hawaii is comprised of a chain of volcanic and coral islands 2,090 miles from San Francisco. Of the 20 islands in the chain, the best known are Hawaii, Oahu, Kauai, and Maui.

Also called the Aloha State and Paradise of the Pacific, Hawaii was first settled by Polynesians about 500 A.D. Other immigrants arrived during the 12th and 13th centuries. Captain James Cook rediscovered the islands in 1778, naming them the Sandwich Islands, and was killed there in 1779.

King Kamehameha I was responsible for uniting the islands under his rule (1795–1819) and his successors made much progress, including the recognition of Hawaii as an independent nation by the United States, Great Britain, and France, when the dynasty ended in 1872. The last native ruler, Queen Liliuokalani, was deposed in 1893, accused of misrule, and Hawaii requested annexation to the United States which was established by joint resolution in 1898. Hawaii was established as a U.S. territory on April 30, 1900.

A port of call for American whalers during the early 19th century, Hawaii was targeted by American missionaries for their zealous efforts to clothe and Christianize the natives. After first visiting the islands in 1820, the missionaries began to arrive in droves, establishing themselves as self-appointing moral police. After convincing the natives that their happy ways of dress and behavior were sinful, many of them settled there and their descendants reaped great fortunes trading the island commodoties of sugar, pineapples, and other crops.

Hawaii is the home of the Hawaiian Islands Bird Reservation at the Leeward Islands and the Hawaii National Park and Haleakala National Park.

$\mathscr{H}$AWAIIAN

Note: Hawaiian names are not divided by gender as most names are used interchangeably for both girls and boys.

Names exclusively female are marked *f*; those exclusively male, *m*.

Name	Meaning
Ahulani	Heavenly shrine
Akela	Form of Adelle, noble
Akoni	Inestimable
Alamea	Ripe or precious Hawaiian
Alana	An offering
Alani	Orange or oahu tree, fragrant
Alaula	Dawn light or sunset glow
Alika	Truthful
Aloha	Love, affection, kindness, greeting
Alohi	Shining or brilliant
Alohilani	Bright sky
Amaui	Thrush, gently dusky bird
Ana	Graceful
Anabela, *f*.	Beautiful and graceful
Anela	Angel or native god
Ani	Beautiful
Aolani	Heavenly cloud
Aulaula	Heavenly seabird
Aulii	Dainty

. . . .

Babara, *f*.	Form of Barbara, stranger

| Balaniki | Form of Blanche, white |
| Bane, *m.* | Son of prophecy or consolation (form of Barney given to a long-awaited child) |

· ·

| Dolore, *f.* | Sorrows |
| Dorisa, *f.* | From the sea |

· ·

Edena, *f.*	Development of Edna
Edi	Rich gift
Elese	Noble
Eli	The highest
Ema	Beloved
Emalia	Industrious
Evalina	Life
Ezera	Help

· ·

| Gladi | Gladiola |

· ·

Haimi	Seeker
Hakulani	Star in heaven
Hale, *m.*	Army ruler
Havika	Beloved
Helena	Light
Hoku	Star
Hokulani	Star in the sky

· ·

| Iao | Name of a star |

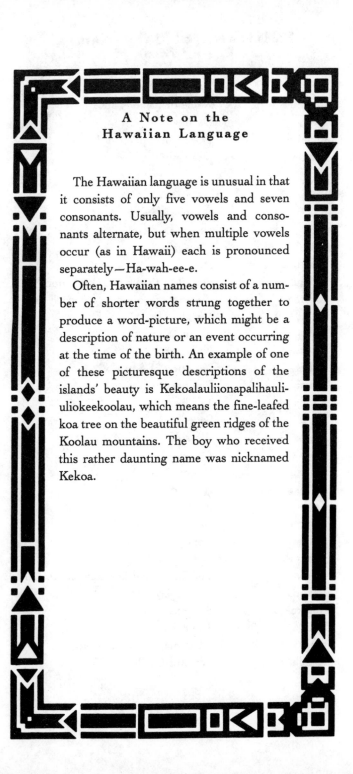

A Note on the
Hawaiian Language

The Hawaiian language is unusual in that
it consists of only five vowels and seven
consonants. Usually, vowels and consonants alternate, but when multiple vowels
occur (as in Hawaii) each is pronounced
separately—Ha-wah-ee-e.

Often, Hawaiian names consist of a number of shorter words strung together to
produce a word-picture, which might be a
description of nature or an event occurring
at the time of the birth. An example of one
of these picturesque descriptions of the
islands' beauty is Kekoalauliionapalihauli-
uliokeekoolau, which means the fine-leafed
koa tree on the beautiful green ridges of the
Koolau mountains. The boy who received
this rather daunting name was nicknamed
Kekoa.

Iaolani	Name of a beautiful star
Inoa	Name or name chant
Ipo	Darling
Iulani	The highest point of heaven
Iwalani	Heavenly sea bird

• •

Kai	Sea or seawater
Kaili	Hawaiian diety
Kaimi	The seeker
Kakalina	Pure
Kakaulani	Placed in the sky (constellation)
Kalama	Flaming torch, wife of King Kamehameha III
Kale	The eastern sky
Kama	Nursling
Kamika	Variation of Smith
Kanani	The beauty
Kanoa	The free one
Kapu	Sacred
Kapua	Blossom
Kapule	A prayer
Kaulana	Famous one
Kawika	Beloved
Keahi	Fire
Kealoha	Beloved
Keiki	Child
Kekapa	The tapa cloth
Kekoa	The fine-leafed koa tree on Koolau
Kekona	Second-born child
Kelekokio	Seahorse
Kelii	The chief
Kiele	Gardenia, or fragrant blossom
Kikilia, *f.*	Form of Cecilia

Kini	Form of Jean, God is gracious
Konane	Bright as moonlight
Kuulei	My lei (garland of flowers)

· ·

Laban	White
Lahela	Form of Rachel, or, Ewe
Laka	Attract or tame (goddess of the hula)
Lana	Buoyant or to float
Lani	Sky or heavenly
Laniuma	Geranium
Lavi	Lion
Lehua	Sacred to the gods, also flower
Lehualani	Sky flower
Lei	Wreath or child
Leilani	Heavenly flower
Leinaala	Path of leis
Lekeke	Ruler (form of Richard)
Lileana	Form of Lillian, lily
Lilia	The lily flower
Lio, *m*	Form of Leo, lion
Liona	Lion, or the sign of Leo
Loe	King (form of roi)
Lokelani	Heavenly rose
Lono, *m.*	God of peace and agriculture
Lulani	The highest point in heaven

· ·

Mahealani	Where heaven is
Mahina	Moon
Makana	Gift or present (from God)
Makani	The wind
Malia	Honey
Malu	Peace

Malulani	Under heaven's protection
Mamo	Saffron flower or yellow bird
Mana	Supernatural powers
Mapelai	Lovable
Mauli	Dark complexion
Mei	Month of May, or "great one"
Meka	Eyes
Mekalani	Heavenly eyes
Mekanani	Beautiful eyes
Mele	A song or poem
Melei	Heavenly flower or song child
Mere	Bitter
Miliama	Bitter
Moana	Ocean

· ·

Nahele	Forest or grove of trees
Namilani	Beautiful heaven
Nani	Form of Ann, beautiful
Nohea	Handsome or beautiful

· ·

Okalani	Of the heavens, or from heaven
Ola	Life or health
Olliana	Oleander
Olu	Gentle

· ·

Palani	Free one
Palila	Bird
Peke	Shining, glorious
Pililani	Close to heaven
Pilis	Lover of horses
Pokii, *f.*	Younger sister

Pua — Flower
Pualani — Heavenly flower (bird of paradise)
Puanani — Beautiful flower
Puni — Wild ginger blossom

....

Rahela, *f.* — Form of Rachael
Roselani — Heavenly rose

....

Silivia — From the forest
Suke — Form of Susan, or lily

....

Ulani — Cheerful

....

Vegenia — Maidenly
Viviana — Lively

....

Wilima — Resolute protector

Hawaiian Celestial Names

Some of the loveliest-sounding Hawaiian names refer to the sky, heaven, or some celestial event. Here are a few examples:

Ahulani: heavenly shrine
Alaula: dawn light sunset glow
Alohilani: bright sky
Aolani: heavenly cloud
Hokulani: star in the sky
Iulani: the highest point of heaven
Kakaulani: placed in the sky
Leilani: heavenly flower

Lani, meaning sky or heavenly, is a component of many longer names, as shown above.